YOU ARE AS YOUNG
AS YOUR SPINE

Editha Hearn

CYRIAX PHYSIOTHERAPIST

M.C.S.P. - ME. - LET. - LONDON

Illustrations by Charlotta Adlerova

GRAMERCY • NEW YORK

0-517-129604
Copyright © MCMLXVII by Editha Hearn
Library Of Congress Catalog Card Number: 66-17431
All rights reserved.
This edition is published by GRAMERCY PUBLISHING COMPANY
a division of CROWN PUBLISHERS, INC.
by arrangement with DOUBLEDAY AND COMPANY
    b c d e f g h
Manufactured in the United States Of America

Contents

Preface

This book is written for all those who suffer from "back-ache," "neck pain," "lumbago," "stiff neck," headache or "migraine"; or "muscular pain," "rheumatic pains," "fibrositis" or "trigger points" in the trunk, "brachial neuritis" in the arm, or "sciatica" in the leg, all of which, 90 percent of the time, are due to slipped discs. Perfect discs in a modern spine are as rare as perfect teeth in a modern mouth. We nearly all suffer at times from the pain of one or more slipped discs, though we may not be ill enough to go to a doctor for treatment or even know our pain is due to a slipped disc. Only very rarely is surgery necessary.

The book is also written for patients who are being or have been treated by their doctors or physiotherapists, to help them understand their infirmity, so that they can co-operate during treatment, and afterward form a lifetime habit of simple prophylaxis against further attacks.

The method of diagnosis and treatment of slipped discs is a recent development in physiotherapy, devised, pioneered, and practiced by Dr. James Cyriax, M.D., F.R.C.P. (London) Orthopedic Physician of St. Thomas's Hospital, London.

His methods of Orthopedic Manipulation and Traction are practiced in my clinic, but this is not an account of the treatment of slipped discs (the same as disc lesions or discopathy) but rather the practical advice which has not been previously written for the layman, but which is so necessary for his recovery, and essential for avoiding a recurrence of this painful disorder.

Many patients have told me how, by using the methods that I have taught them, they have helped a friend, or a member of the family, to get rid of chronic tiredness or recurring "rheumatism" or "fibrositis" in the neck, shoulder, or lower back. This means that others with a minor disc lesion could also cure themselves without any treatment other than the Corrective Movements in Chapter 2 and the Exercises in Chapter 9 simply by changing bad spinal habits, according to the directions in this book.

Others, usually those with a history of chronic general discopathy ("muscular rheumatism all over the body"), having been instructed by some other patient, not always correctly, in the simple routine outlined here, have improved considerably before asking their doctor to send them for treatment to effect complete recovery. It seems to me that these patients have needed fewer sessions than those who have had no previous instruction.

Then there are patients who, because of the debility and the nervous depression that so often accompany a disc lesion, are in no mood to receive instruction; in fact, they resent it. They would, I believe, accept it if they could read about it quietly at home at their leisure. Moreover, the physiotherapist herself cannot always be at her best with every patient; she is but human. There are those who, by their obvious interest, inspire her to an enthusiastic discourse. There are others who, by their apathy or even antagonism, reduce instruction to an insipid minimum.

Other patients who have had the operation for disc removal (laminectomy) come for treatment after another attack, wishing to avoid further surgery. They blame the surgeon for an unsuccessful operation. This is most unjust. First, they were warned that the operation is a delicate one, the result of which cannot be guaranteed, and second, I am often able to point out that the operation was a complete success, but that their pain, though it may feel the same or has shifted only slightly, is not caused by the same disc as before. Having had one disc removed does not guarantee immunity against protrusion of another, and the fact that someone has had one disc lesion, unprovoked by a serious accident, points to the fact that the cartilaginous rims of the discs in the adjacent joints of the spine are probably already damaged, though not yet causing symptoms.

The orthopedic surgeon is far too busy to do other than briefly sketch the prophylaxis to be followed after the operation, and since the treatment of disc lesions is comparatively new, the patient has no other source of information. This book then should also help those who, having been unfortunate enough to need laminectomy, wish to learn how to avoid returning to the habits which made the operation necessary in the first place.

Acknowledgments

My own patients, I think, have helped me most to write this book, by asking what they should do or avoid doing, and by describing how they overcame certain difficulties. All their experiences are here to help others.

My sincere thanks to Mrs. Heddy Schott for her unstinted collaboration.

Figures from the *Text Book of Orthopaedic Medicine*, Vol. I, are reproduced by kind permission of Dr. Cyriax. When I studied this specialized course, postgraduately, at St. Thomas's from 1950 to 1952, his *Text Book of Orthopaedic Medicine*, Vol. I, was then being written. It was only published in 1954 (Cassell & Company, London), when for the first time diagnosis of disc lesions in all parts of the spinal column was expounded. This was a period of intense activity for Dr. Cyriax and his helpers. I had the great good fortune to work under these outstanding pioneers, Mrs. Skillern and Miss Moffatt, and I owe them much for patiently introducing me to a work so intensely interesting, and at the same time so revolutionary. I am proud that now in some small way I can contribute to the New Era of Physiotherapy by writing for the layman who suffers so frequently from this demoralizing disease, and who knows so little about it.

To my chief Dr. Cyriax my deep and eternal gratitude—only a physiotherapist like myself, who after years of work has had the privilege of entering the New School, can feel the satisfaction of abandoning palliative measures in preference to those which are logical and give real results. Anyone who practices these methods gains the esteem of his patients and great contentment in his work.

1: Anatomy of the Spine

The spinal column is made up of strong bones, the vertebrae, almost impossible to break, except by direct blow of a heavy object, a fall, or an accident which bends, twists, or crushes the spine immoderately. In between the movable vertebrae, however (except between the first and second cervical), lie the shock absorbers—called intervertebral discs.

These discs are more clearly seen on looking at the spine from the front, and appear to be made of cartilage as is found lining the bones of the other joints of the body (Fig. 1).

Each disc in reality consists of two parts, a fibrocartilaginous ring and a pulpy center rather like boiled crab meat. Each varies in size and shape to fit the joint and is attached to the rim of the joint (Fig. 2). This is surrounded by a capsular covering reinforced in front and behind by ligaments (like elastic bands), which help hold the discs in position (Fig. 3). Behind the joint, in a closed bony canal, runs the spinal cord protected by a thick covering called the dura mater. From the spinal cord, nerves are given off in pairs opposite the intervertebral space, carrying motor impulses to muscles and sensory signals both to and from the brain. In profile (Fig. 4) a normal spine shows two slight curves, the cervical and the lumbar lordoses. Each joint is placed at a slightly different angle, and only by maintaining these lordoses can each disc be held without strain in the center of its joint and in alignment

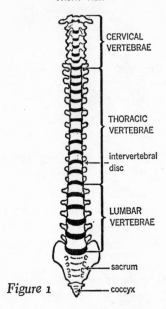

Figure 1

- CERVICAL VERTEBRAE
- THORACIC VERTEBRAE
- intervertebral disc
- LUMBAR VERTEBRAE
- sacrum
- coccyx

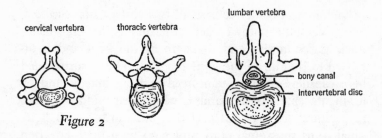

cervical vertebra   thoracic vertebra   lumbar vertebra

bony canal
intervertebral disc

Figure 2

with the others. When the curves are either continually exaggerated, or allowed to disappear, the body weight is increased on some part of the perimeter of the disc, tending to break it away from the rim and crack it. It may crack in one place or more; sometimes in many. With increasing peripheral pressure (compression strain) together with

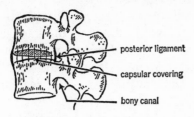

posterior ligament

capsular covering

bony canal

Figure 3

·SIDE VIEW

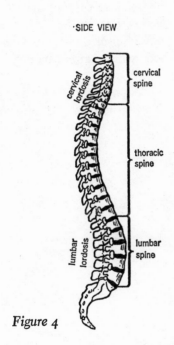

cervical
lordosis

cervical
spine

thoracic
spine

lumbar
lordosis

lumbar
spine

Figure 4

movement of the joints these cracks begin to open, and allow part of the rim to protrude outside the joint (Fig. 5). Now the disc has slipped.

Sometimes a piece of cartilage between two cracks becomes loose and protrudes (Fig. 6).

Sometimes the pulp begins to ooze out between the

cracks and forms a herniated protrusion (Fig. 7). If the protrusion takes place toward the front of the joint away from the spinal cord and nerves, *there are no symptoms* because there is no sensitive nerve in front of the joint, but the damage has begun and the ring weakened, leading to the possibility of further damage to the posterior half. If the break is posterior and cartilage or pulp protrudes into the spinal canal, *there are still no symptoms until the pressure is transmitted through the capsule and the posterior ligament onto the sensitive dura mater or the nerve roots.* This may happen at any level of the spine. There is practically no pain in the body which cannot be imitated by disc pressure.

A *slipped disc (disc lesion) is important only when it produces symptoms.* You do not even know you have one

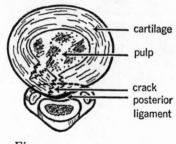

cartilage

pulp

crack
posterior
ligament

Figure 5

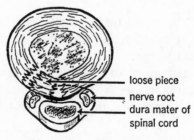

loose piece
nerve root
dura mater of
spinal cord

Figure 6

unless it does. Usually at first the symptoms are slight, often merely tiredness, e.g. at the back of the neck or between the shoulder blades; sometimes a dull ache in the lower back after strenuous work which then disappears after resting.

More seldom these pains begin distally, perhaps in the buttock, thigh, calf, or foot or in the shoulder, forearm, or fingers. These warnings are usually dismissed as "rheumatism" or "trigger points" or "fibrositis." Many valuable months are sometimes lost in treating these as separate entities, whereas if the spinal joint containing the broken disc is manipulated, these symptoms usually disappear in one to five treatments. If pain in a limb is caused by disc pressure, what has happened is that the protrusion has shifted to one side, or the crack may have formed in a

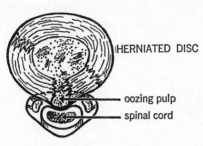

HERNIATED DISC

— oozing pulp
— spinal cord

Figure 7

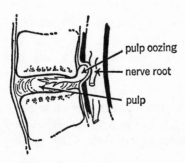

— pulp oozing
— nerve root
— pulp

Figure 8

lateral posterior position. If so, the pressure is on the dural covering of the root of one of the spinal nerves leading away from the spinal cord (Fig. 8).

Very often through some advantageous movement or position the disc begins to move back into place and ceases to exert pressure; hence the pain disappears.

But one day when the joint is forced unduly open at the back or held in that position for long, the pain recurs, this time with real intensity. Then the patient may be bent either forward, or over to one side, which if a lumbar lesion is present gives one a feeling that one leg is shorter than the other. He may also feel other symptoms, such as pain or pull in one or both legs, or "nervous cystitis," which means the patient urinates too frequently or has difficulty in urinating. He may also feel numbness or pins and needles in one or both legs or feet. Very rarely does he have all these symptoms at once, but he may have one or more of them. Now he visits his doctor. If he tells him he has a disc lesion, he forgets he has had the early warning signs of "rheumatism" and thinks the disc broke at the moment when the intense pain began.

It is not possible to know when a disc breaks, only when it slips and exerts pressure on a sensitive structure. You may have an accident and except for some bruising, feel nothing until some weeks afterward. But you are far more likely to break a disc in a less spectacular way, by prolonged, continuous, and unnecessary ill-treatment of the spine. It may be that some months or even years later quite a simple accident initiates displacement. "Rheumatism" is only another name for pain, as is "lumbago" (pain felt in the lumbar region), "sciatica" (pain felt along the sciatic nerve), "torticollis" (pain felt in the muscles of the neck), and "fibrositis" (pain felt in the muscles of the back). But none of these words indicate the *cause* of the pain, and 90 percent of all pains in the neck or back, whether or not later radiating to the front of the trunk or into a limb, arise from disc lesions. The other 10 percent have other causes, most of them more serious, though not more *painful* than a disc lesion.

On being told by your doctor that you have a slipped disc, do not think you have some rare and frightening new disease which needs an immediate operation. *Disc lesions (either slipped cartilage or oozing pulp) are the most common cause of spine trouble,* their importance varying according to how large the protrusion is, and how long before it is subjected to logical treatment.

Between 80 and 90 percent of all adults at one time or another suffer from one or more disc lesions. Sometimes a short but severe attack may be ended by the piece of protruding disc slipping back into place. If so, pain and deformity disappear and there is no need for treatment, but the prevention of renewed displacement is important.

If the symptoms persist or are often repeated, displacement should be reduced as soon as possible by manipulation or traction, otherwise the most favorable moment is lost and later treatment will be more prolonged and complicated, and may even fail. Furthermore, a disc lesion is hardly ever serious in the beginning even though it may cause acute pain. (The term *"reduced"* means put back into place.)

2: Treatment

When a disc is damaged and moves out of place, causing pain, it should be replaced where it belongs (reduced) by manipulation or traction as soon as possible, by a doctor or physiotherapist.

MANIPULATION

Spinal manipulations mean movements of the joints of the spine, performed by the hands of the manipulator. Osteopaths and chiropractors manipulate and each have their own methods. The orthopedic medical manipulations developed by Dr. James Cyriax, M.D., M.R.C.P., Orthopedic Physician of St. Thomas's Hospital, London, are quite different. They are a series of manipulations done in a certain sequence and with due precaution to insure the best possible results. The patient is asked to cooperate by doing a number of movements after each manipulation to help the physiotherapist assess improvement. She can also tell by this means when to avoid any particular manipulation.

All Dr. Cyriax's physiotherapists are taught this assessment by diagnostic movements. They also note if a secondary protrusion is present, since a movement of one joint of the spine will affect another in which the disc is already cracked. This analysis is not a doctor's examination, it is merely complementary to it and necessary if the physiotherapist is to do her best for the patient. She should also have access to any available X rays, since these will often suggest where to look for complications during treatment.

TRACTION

Traction is used mainly for pulpy protrusions, but as cartilage and pulp often move together it may become necessary to change from manipulation to traction, or vice versa. The Cyriax traction table is designed to treat the patient lying down. Traction pulls the joints apart, thus allowing more intervertebral space for re-entry of the protruding part of the disc. The lengthening of the joint capsule and the ligaments promotes a centripetal force pushing the disc inward. It also creates a suction which further helps the re-entry movement. Since the upper pull is from a waistcoat around the chest and the lower from a belt around the hips, it is sometimes possible for a strong man to endure a pull of up to two hundred pounds for half an hour or more in comparative comfort. Each patient helps to decide how much pull is right for him and for how long he can stand it.

Treatment by traction usually takes longer than by manipulation, as it is used when the disc protrusion is larger and therefore more difficult to reduce. Not until the spinal analysis has been completed is it possible to decide whether traction is the best method.

When manipulative treatment is required for a simple protrusion, one to five sessions are usual; if traction, five to ten sessions. In a case of general discopathy, which means protrusions from several discs, manipulation ranges from five to eight sessions, and in very longstanding cases a further attendance once a week for about five weeks may be necessary. Early cases nearly always get well more quickly as there are fewer complications.

ORTHOPEDIC CORSET

If treatment by manipulation or traction is delayed for

too long it may be necessary to wear an orthopedic corset once the protrusion has been reduced, but it is generally reserved for those cases in which the ligaments have lost their elasticity after years of being stretched by the protruding disc, or the patient has muscles so hopelessly weak that they cannot be re-educated within reasonable time to take over control. By contrast, when a corset is applied *instead* of reducing the disc, it is not very helpful. It can prevent further protrusion, but rarely entirely banishes pain of the current protrusion.

PLASTER CAST

A plaster cast is necessary only after an operation of bone graft of a spinal joint, or after laminectomy while waiting for a surgical corset. A plaster cast applied *before* reduction or operation serves only to prevent further protrusion, but cannot help reduction unless the lesion is so slight that it would have reduced itself.

REST IN BED

Rest in bed nearly always helps. If a patient is too ill to attend for manipulation or traction, he should remain in bed under his doctor's care with analgesic injections and, when possible, lying for spells on heat in the Supported Position described in Chapter 5. However, recumbency takes a long time to become effective. As soon as the patient is well enough to get up, he will improve more rapidly by manipulation or traction.

Foot traction applied while the patient is bedridden simply increases his discomfort and does not hasten recovery.

OPERATION

Some disc protrusions not treated in the early stages become so large that they cannot be reduced either by manipulation or traction. An operation is then necessary for removing the disc (laminectomy). This operation is performed less frequently nowadays, as the results have proved less successful than was hoped. There are cases in which there is no choice, but relapses are not uncommon. Sometimes only the pulp and the damaged part of the cartilage is removed; later, another portion of cartilage may protrude. Some surgeons remove the whole disc and apply a bone graft to keep the joint firm; however, the joint above or below is strained because of this and a new disc may be damaged, causing relapse. Moreover, since treatment by Cyriax manipulations and traction has become more widely known, the necessity for operation has been reduced to one or two in every hundred cases.

SPONTANEOUS CURE

There are then some few cases in which operation is imperative. Nevertheless, if the patient has been suffering for many months with a disc which cannot be reduced by manipulation or traction, operation should be deferred if there is an appreciable chance of spontaneous cure. This will be explained to him by his doctor. While waiting for this, it is often necessary to have an epidural injection into the spine to reduce pain and keep him comfortable pending recuperation.

CURE

The disc itself, once broken, cannot heal. Once mature, it is cut off from all blood supply, like the cartilage in other joints, or the ends of the nails. This means all nourishment to make strong healthy discs is supplied from the time a human being is an embryo until he is about nine or ten years old. Disc lesions are uncommon in children but unhappily *do* occur as early as the age of nine or ten years. Later than this, the disc probably cannot be supplied with building or mending material, though the ligaments and muscles can, and these will help to keep it in place. Remember, however, a disc in place, although broken, causes no symptoms. Thus, although there is no cure, you can, by having it reduced or having it removed, arrive at the same result—freedom from pain. If the disc is reduced, you must learn to keep it where it belongs. After operation you must defend the other joints of the spine so that other protrusions will not occur.

You can be quite sure that having had a protrusion from one joint means the cartilage is also weak in other joints and is probably already cracked.

Keeping the broken disc in position is not as difficult as it sounds. First there is the shape of the joint. In profile an X ray shows that the two surfaces of the vertebrae forming the joint are concave, so that the disc is rather like an oyster protected in its shell. You cannot see the disc itself on the X ray photograph, because unlike bone it is translucent, but by showing the shape and angulation of the joint, the picture nevertheless gives very important information as to what is happening to the disc.

It also shows how much compensatory calcification exists. *This calcification until recently was thought to be the cause of pain in the spine. Now it is recognized as beneficial, being a defense mechanism tending to stabilize the joints in which there is a* broken disc (Fig. 9).

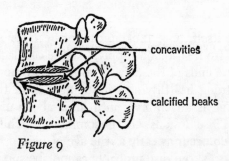

concavities

calcified beaks

Figure 9

Thirdly, there is the strong posterior ligament holding the disc from pushing backward into the spinal canal. And lastly there are the muscles which can be trained to hold the joints in their proper position.

To prevent a recurrence of protrusion you will want to know:

1. How to carry out simple movements which initiate the centralizing movements of the protruding part of a disc. These are called Corrective Movements and are performed at the three parts of the spine—cervical, thoracic, and lumbar. They can hardly be described as exercises since the movements, though begun by muscles, are continued by impetus and gravity. Indeed, strenuous exercises are *not* indicated; they are definitely unwise.

2. How to keep the joints in position by control of posture (i.e., how to maintain both cervical and lumbar curves as well as possible. It really *does* matter how you lie, how you sit, how you stand and walk, and how you bend and carry weights. Moreover, the right way is the graceful way and one which we admire in others, whether they have come by it naturally or by training. There exists a real relation between a good posture and a healthy body free of rheumatism, lumbago, sciatica, fibrositis, brachial neuritis, intercostal neuritis, chronic headaches, migraine, and the many other ills which so often have their origin in disc pressure. (See Chapters 3 through 7.)

3. How to avoid extra compression strain so that the weight of the body does not force the cracked disc backward (see Chapter 8).

THE CORRECTIVE MOVEMENTS

(a) *The Cervical Spine*

The cervical is the most mobile part of the spine. The required movements are: backward and forward (Fig. 10), twisting to each side (Fig. 11), and then bending to each side (Fig. 12). Each movement is repeated at least twice, with the head coming back to the anatomical position without pausing, with the slow, smooth rhythm of a pendulum. Once you find the movements do not cause undue pain, they will be more effective if you imagine your head attached to the body by a flexible wire, and flick the head gently in each direction.

Should there be much pain, limitation, or stiffness at first, use the hands to cup the jaws and lift the weight of the head upward off the body (but not backward); and tilt, twist, and side-bend the head passively (Fig. 13). This allows space whereby the displaced fragment of disc, which is blocking the joint, can return more easily. Afterward you

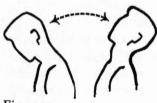

Figure 10

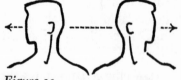

Figure 11

will probably find you can continue with the active movements more freely.

All these movements are easier after a hot shower or bath, or applying a very hot wet towel to the back of the neck, since the muscles are then relaxed and the compression on the joints lessened.

Sometimes there is a clean "click" or "plop" which is probably a fragment of cartilage moving advantageously inwards, as this brings relief. The sound of rubble or sand shows that the disc is much damaged.

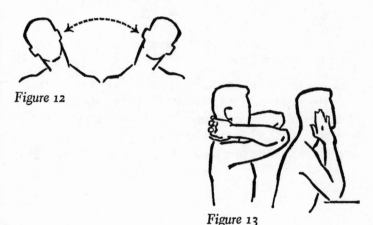

Figure 12

Figure 13

The movements should be repeated until there is some relief from pain and stiffness, or at least until the unpleasant grinding sound is diminished.

(b) *The Thoracic Spine*

With elbows bent, raise the arms to the shoulder level (but do not hunch the shoulders) and then press them backward (Fig. 14). *When they can go no further*, gently jerk the chest forward (Fig. 15). Repeat two or three times and try for a rewarding click.

The arms may be bent or extended, whichever is found easier. This movement does much to counteract the tendency to round shoulders or a stoop as one grows older.

Figure 14   Figure 15

(c) *The Lumbar Spine*

Place the thumbs on either side of and close to the spine, with the abdominal muscles held in; then rock backward (Fig. 16). As you do so, press the thumbs firmly into the back at each backward movement, applying counterpressure twice in the same place (Fig. 17). Then move them

Figure 16   Figure 17

downward for about one-half inch and repeat until you reach the end of the lumbar spine.

Repeat a, b, and c—this takes roughly one minute—as often as necessary to obtain at least some relief. These

Corrective Movements should be done whenever the spine begins to feel tired, to stiffen up, or to ache, and at any time that the pain seems to be increasing. There is no limit for how often you should do them, or how often you should repeat them unless it is "the more the better." Do them at least three times a day.

Experience will teach you which movements help most and these you can repeat more often; but do not forget they are *all* necessary, since the spine works as a whole, one part affecting the others.

When you first begin to do them, do not expect immediate results. Later on they will often banish pain immediately, hence it is reasonable to believe that they will shorten considerably the time which any disc pain would otherwise continue.

When symptoms have ceased, and you are well again, you should still continue the Corrective Movements as a prophylactic measure and make them a life habit.

Having the protruding part of a disc reduced by manipulation or traction is rather like going to the dentist. He does the fillings which are necessary, but your teeth are not "cured." You brush them if possible three times a day to prevent further caries in the same ones or in others. As to your spine, even when there is no more pain you should also do the Corrective Movements at least three times a day, to prevent displacement of the same disc or of others.

You should do them (1) on getting up in the morning, because the perfect bed does not exist, and because during the night you may unconsciously sleep in positions very trying to the spine; (2) again before lying down during the day for ten minutes to break compression strain, so as to get the full benefit of the short rest; (3) before going to sleep, because all through the day you unavoidably bend the spine forward in eating, writing, getting into a car, cutting the toenails, etc., etc., and you should cancel the effect of these repeated flexions at the end of each day.

3: How to Lie

1. A *Hard Bed* (Fig. 18)

In the past, and unfortunately even today, one of the greatest errors in treating back cases is to make the patient lie on a hard flat surface. Since the spine is not thus shaped, this is unreasonable, but the idea originated from the desire to correct a sagging bed. *A hard bed, or worse still the floor, must therefore be condemned.* First there is an exaggeration of the extension of the joints, but as the muscles relax they fall into flexion and any broken disc can move outward onto the dura mater.

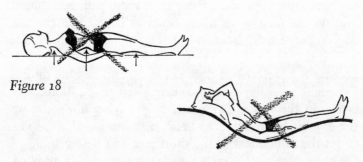

Figure 18

Figure 19

Sometimes someone may have a very large piece of protruding disc which can only be accommodated with the joint forced open posteriorly. This is why he may feel more comfortable on a hard bed. However, this position will not help the patient toward recovery but rather delay it.

2. A *Sagging Bed* (Fig. 19)

A sagging bed is even worse as it causes *immediate* flexion of the spinal joints. As the muscles relax, flexion of the spine increases even more than when the sufferer lies on a hard flat surface. This is what doctors have been rightly trying to correct. However, the hard bed is not the solution; a firm *base* is what is needed, with a soft mattress to contour the curves of the body. A sagging bed is condemned.

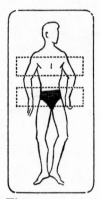

Figure 20

If the *base* is of springs, either a network or the more luxurious box springs, supporting any form of mattress, hair, wool, foam, or more springs, there is always danger of sagging. *This can be easily and inexpensively prevented by placing crosswise*, between the mattress and its spring base, and under the area on which the trunk of the body lies, two or three boards about 9 to 12 inches wide, and in length 1 foot less than the width of the bed. This allows the springs to give, but not sag, and does not damage the hands during bedmaking (Fig. 20).

For a double bed the boards should go across under the bodies of both sleepers, still leaving the 6 inch space on either side. The other partner will not notice the difference, as the comfort of the bed is unaltered, but he may notice after a few days that he sleeps better and seems more rested in the morning. *What is good for a damaged back is also good for a normal one.*

Your bed may be adequate at home, but when traveling, you must beware of the bed which behaves like a hammock. Make shift with provisional supports, boards from the sides of a wooden box, a cupboard shelf, the wooden slatted foot stand normally in use under a shower, or anything else practical. If this prophylaxis is neglected, the chances are that for the first day or two you will feel only a tiredness or a vague ache, but later this will be followed by pain.

Figure 21

3. A Good Bed (Fig. 21)

What one needs in lying down is a support which contours the body curves and, without sagging, holds them in the proper anatomical position. There are various combinations: (1) A spring mattress on a slatted wooden base. Since the nature of springs is to sag, they must be checked from time to time. (2) This also applies to the sofa bed. (3) A thick foam rubber mattress on a hard base. (4) A thinner foam rubber mattress two to three inches thick on a spring mattress which is too hard for comfort. Any spring mattress or sofa bed is improved by this extra layer. (5) A spring mattress or box springs with slats in between as described under "sagging bed."

Though some manufacturers have come near to it, there does not exist a perfect bed which will exactly contour the body, or give additional support to the curves when most needed. This is why we use pillows, as well as a mattress.

Pillows should be soft, not hard, especially under the head and neck. The most comfortable to use are made of swan's-down, not too fully stuffed, or foam rubber. Some foam pillows are too resilient and will not let the head relax, but keep pushing it up off the bed. These are better for under the knees or in a smaller edition under the lumbar curve. You will need at least three pillows for your bed.

LYING ON THE BACK

Not many people sleep in this position nor is it necessary for them to do so. However, it is one that is usually comfortable before turning onto the side, and one which is most helpful in spinal treatment. You need a soft pillow which not only supports the head but fills in the nape of the neck without pushing the head forward; one under the lumbar curve, and a large one under the knees, to relieve further strain in the small of the back. This is the

SUPPORTED POSITION

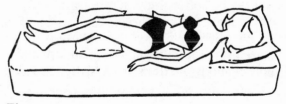

Figure 22

Supported Position (Fig. 22). Lying in this position favors the return of any protruding portion of disc into the joint, and one can best apply heat with either electric pad or hot-water bottle to the areas from which the pain originates. Heat relaxes the trunk muscles which are contracted by the pain, and so allows more intervertebral space for re-entry of the broken portion of disc. The electric pad must be placed on the supporting cushion, though a hot-water bottle with sufficient water and with the air expelled may be used alone as it also furnishes the support needed. The heat must be as much as can be borne without dis-comfort, so put almost boiling water in the bottle and wrap it up well before applying. In times of pain one can stay in this position for an hour or more.

If (as may occasionally happen) the pain increases, do not stay long on your back, because, although this is the best theoretical position for the spine, *your* spine may not be comfortable if the bulge of the disc is so great that it is impossible to hold the affected joint normally.

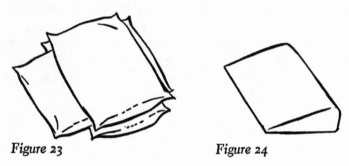

Figure 23   Figure 24

The pillows or bottles must not exaggerate the cervical and lumbar curves, nor will they be comfortable if they do, and must be adjusted to each case. No one but you can properly arrange yours. Depending on the depth of your curves and the softness of the mattress, they may vary greatly. If you are quite comfortable, you may like to begin your sleep with the heat, turning over only on first awakening.

If you normally sleep in this position, remove the heat when you have had enough, but do not sleep without at least the cervical and lumbar supports. You are advised then to rest in this positon, but not required to *sleep* on the back.

When reading in bed, on one's back, the head must be high enough to see the book properly, and you can make a comfortable gradual inclination by arranging more pillows, first crosswise and then longwise (Fig. 23), beginning under the shoulders but still maintaining the neck support. This ramp may be as high as desired, especially for sufferers from heart disease or asthma, and can be used for sleeping so long as the curves are properly supported. Some prefer a wedge-shaped foam rubber base under the pillows (Fig. 24), and others a board which rests on the low headpiece of the bed.

Each bed will present its own problem, but this can be overcome by any enthusiastic reader-in-bed or television fan. What must be avoided is propping the back of the head on a thick head roll or pillow (Fig. 25) or the back of the bed, or—on the other hand—lying on a low pillow and unconsciously lifting the head off the neck support in an effort to see the book. Not only are the cervical and upper thoracic joints pulled open posteriorly, but there is a remote effect on the joints of the lumbar spine. In some cases of large disc protrusion, this neck flexion pulls on the dura mater, stretching it over the protrusion, causing further pain in the area of the referred pain, e.g. the buttock or the leg.

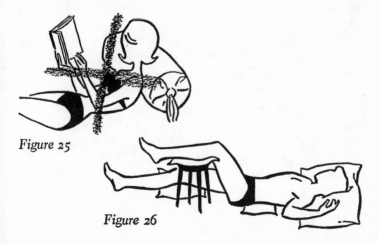

Figure 25

Figure 26

Sometimes in acute sciatica even slight neck flexion of one supporting pillow is enough to increase the pain in the leg, and the supporting knee pillow is not enough. The patient may have to flex the knee much more to relieve the pull, either by putting more pillows under the knee on the affected side, or holding it bent up to his abdomen or supporting it on a cushioned stool placed on the bed (Fig. 26).

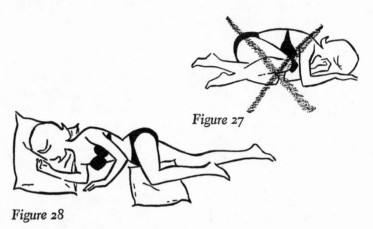

Figure 27

Figure 28

ON THE SIDE

When the sleeper lies on the side, the most usual position chosen for sleep, the anatomical alignment of the spine must still be maintained.

First see that you do not sleep rolled up into a ball. Some psychoanalysts say that this is the position of one who is afraid to face life and prefers the embryonic position with its subconscious memories of warmth and protection (Fig. 27). No doubt this is true, but I think many people who otherwise sleep "bravely" awake on a very cold night to find their feet drawn up to avoid the iciness at the bottom of the bed. So if you suffer from cold feet and yet become too warm with many covers, wear socks on a cold night.

The cervical curve is maintained by holding the chin in the normal position, i.e. parallel with the foot of the bed, and not bent forward on the chest.

The lumbar curve is held by stretching out one leg, usually the lower. The other may then be bent as little or as much as required for complete relaxation and supported by the pillow (which was under the knees in the supine position). This prevents the uncomfortable feeling of falling forward, exaggerated if the hips are large, and avoids rotation of the joints of the spine (Fig. 28). Once you have become accustomed to this position, it will prove very comfortable.

It is also important that the cervical joints have proper support at the side and do not sag open. A soft pillow will fit snugly into the side of the neck and support the head in alignment with the body; if your shoulders are broad you may need another one or more underneath it.

Some are proud that they use a very low pillow or none at all, but in this case the head falls out of alignment (Fig. 29). If it is too high, the pillow forces the head upward (Fig. 30).

If, though of the right height, it begins under the shoulders instead of under the side of the neck—it also causes faulty alignment (Fig. 31). Since beds and bodies differ, the proper height of the pillow or pillows can only be verified by seeing oneself in a mirror while lying in what feels like the correct position. Very rarely is a pillow needed under the waist; only if the hips are large and the waist very narrow.

ure 29

Figure 30

Figure 31

ON THE FRONT

This is not a suitable position in which to sleep. Very often it relieves the lumbar or low thoracic disc pain, holding the joints in good alignment. However, the head is twisted to one side for breathing, which means that the cervical and upper thoracic joints are out of alignment (Fig. 32). If the cartilage is broken in one joint of the spine, the chances are that it has a tendency to be weak in other joints too and can be further broken or forced out of position by faulty alignment.

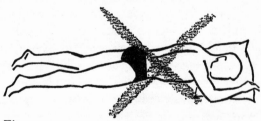

Figure 32

While this is a useful position in which to apply heat to the back either by sunbathing or at home with a radiant heat lamp or an electric pad or hot-water bottle kept in position by a pillow and some heavy books—it is not wise to sleep thus for hours.

If this is the only comfortable position for sleep during

the active phase of a disc lesion, then of course use it, but afterward the habit should be broken. Many have found for themselves that this position will, for instance, bring on one of their cervical disc symptoms, such as headache, giddiness, or pins and needles or numbness in the hand. Another reason for using a pillow under the knee in side lying is that if you turn over onto prone lying the pillow becomes uncomfortable and wakes you before too much time has been spent in this position. Some people are distressed to find that at first they invariably wake in the prone position even if corrected each time, but with patience even the subconscious mind can be trained.

It may seem an exaggeration to write so much about the body position in bed, but it is very important. Perhaps in the future we shall sleep floating in liquid kept at a comfortable temperature. When you have a very painful disc lesion it is often very difficult to get into a comfortable position in bed, or, even more important, not to wake feeling worse in the morning. It is no good doing everything possible during the day to look after the spine and maybe having treatment, only to undo all this good during the average eight to ten hours one is supposed to be resting or sleeping. You cannot be entirely responsible for your position during sleep, but you can begin the night properly and if you are a very restless sleeper, more so because of your present pain, you can during the critical period of your disc trouble do what many patients have discovered for themselves—tuck a small pillow under the cord of your pajamas or tie it in position over your nightdress so that it is always supporting the lumbar curve as you turn on your back. Nature makes the body move into different positions during the night.

Many women suffer from mild backache with pain in the legs after intercourse. If a gynecological examination proves negative, the cause is often due to a mild lumbar disc lesion which does not cause trouble except when the spine is forced into flexion by sagging into a soft mattress. A pillow in the lumbar curve is probably all that is needed. Sex books state that a woman feels more pleasure when thus supported. This may be partly due to the fact that she is no longer unconsciously concerned with resulting backache and discomfort.

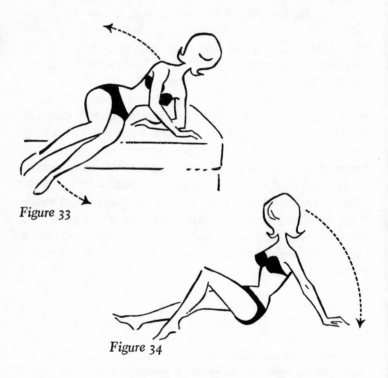

Figure 33

Figure 34

Getting in and out of bed should be a coordinated movement, the knees slightly bent and the head and back kept in a straight line, supported by the hands or elbows. The legs must not be stretched out, nor should the neck be forced forward on the body (Fig. 33, 34). The "rules" of lying do not only apply in bed. Whenever you lie you need support of some kind.

Lying on the Beach, i.e. a hard surface, you should help contour the curves by using either air or plastic pillows, or a rolled towel or bathing wrap, etc. If the only towel is already in use at the neck, a small mound of sand can be used under the lumbar curve; the same effect can be obtained by scooping out a shallow trough for the buttocks. This is an old trick known to early truck drivers who had to sleep on the roadside on long journeys, and who found they developed backache unless they did so. (It also serves for the hips when lying on the side.) There is no need for any support under the knees—one or both can be drawn up for comfort.

Lying on the Grass is slightly more comfortable but use a sweater or convenient tuft of grass for the back, and your hands under your neck (Fig. 35).

Figure 35

Lying in Water presents no problem. Even in a bath the water is sufficiently buoyant to protect the curves for the short time. In sea water, because of its great density, one is protected in any position by a wonderful mattress of water and millions of water pillows which really do contour the body.

Lying on the Sofa. If you like to lie on a sofa for your ten-minute rest, or reading, or looking at T.V., you should keep a collection of soft cushions at hand to make your ramp and to put under the lumbar curve (Fig. 36). If you lie on the side, one cushion between the back of the sofa and your lumbar curve gives a very comfortable support. Do not use the arm of the sofa for abruptly raising the head.

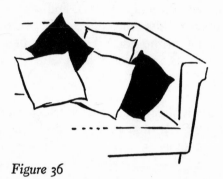

Figure 36

Deck Chairs and similar porch chairs are like a sagging bed, bending the spine forward *unless* you use a pillow in the curves. As this is a half-sitting position, if there is a footrest see that it allows the knees to bend (Fig. 37). Many people come back from a summer holiday spent "resting" in a deck chair only to develop lumbago or sciatica, or feeling more tired than before their holiday.

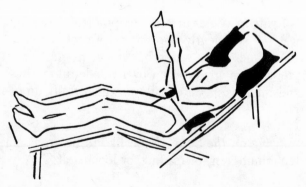

Figure 37

Figure 38

A *Hammock.* Few people, unless they are sailors, know how to use one (Fig. 38). The South American Indian lies diagonally across to sleep, instinctively avoiding too much sag. It is not the best support for a weak back, but if a disc sufferer must use one, he should follow the Indians' example and also remember his supporting cushions.

4: How to Sit

Even when you are correctly seated, flexion at the hips pulls on the lumbar joints and diminishes the normal lordosis. Since the weight on the spine is the same as in standing, and in the ordinary sitting position the joints are more open posteriorly, most lumbar disc sufferers find that either sitting increases their pain, or if the protrusion takes place more slowly, there is pain or at least difficulty and stiffness on getting up after sitting for any length of time. Some sufferers even get up bent over in flexion and then slowly straighten up to the erect position.

Figure 39

SITTING WITHOUT BACK SUPPORT

The longer one sits, the more the joints tend to sag open

42

posteriorly as the muscles tire. To avoid this, one should lift the chest out of the abdomen, gently contract the abdominal and buttock muscles, and bring the weight slightly forward (Fig. 39). For a short time this is adequate, but if you are tired, it helps to lean the forearm or elbow on the arm of the seat, or if it is a low seat without arms, on your own thigh (Fig. 40).

Figure 40

SITTING WITH A BACK SUPPORT

A back support prevents a tired lumbar spine from sagging into flexion; hence chairs were invented. The buttocks should be placed well back against the support and, as before, the chest must be lifted out of the abdomen and the muscles of the abdomen and buttocks slightly contracted. On leaning back, if you find you can pass a hand behind the lumbar lordosis, because of the shape of the chair, this space should be filled with a comfortable pillow appropriate in size, beginning *above* the buttocks.

A GOOD CHAIR

To be comfortable, a chair should have its back support

practically upright, neither hollowed nor too slanted. It may be padded or have a pillow to support the lumbar curve. Sometimes there is a gap in the lower part of the back rest which allows the buttocks room; the padded portion will then fit well into the lumbar curve and no cushion is needed (Fig. 41).

Figure 41

Figure 42

AN ARMCHAIR

An armchair is comfortable if it is softly padded to contour the back, but may still need a cushion. The arms should be high enough to allow the elbows or forearms to rest on them, taking some of the weight off the spine (Fig. 42).

MODERN CHAIRS

Unfortunately, manufacturers are catering to the mass demand for chairs which *appear* to be streamlined and smart, without worrying much whether they are functional or comfortable. They are nearly all either (a) too deep or (b) slanted too much backward, and very often combine both these defects. The chairs designed for the more exclusive manufacturers combine both beauty and comfort.

(a) *Too Deep a Chair*

Chairs should not be too deep since this does not allow the buttocks to touch the backrest, and any pillow for the lumbar curve will slide down behind the buttocks (Fig. 43). The normal lordosis is then lost, the joints sag open, and the broken disc slowly oozes backward; not sufficiently perhaps to bring on pain, but enough to cause tiredness, which is its forerunner. When confronted, while visiting, with an armchair or sofa too deep to lean against, you can sometimes, by sitting on one leg, get back far enough to support the buttocks. If not, you can turn sideways and use the arm of the chair as a backrest (Fig. 44). On a sofa,

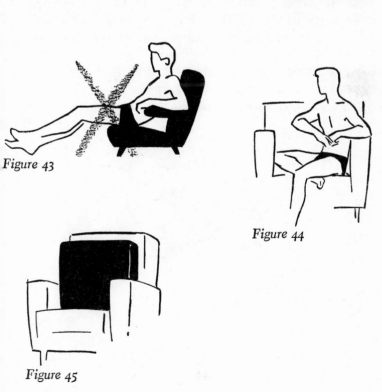

Figure 43

Figure 44

Figure 45

this is a particularly useful position, enabling you to face the person to whom you are speaking without remaining in a twisted position which affects not only the lumbar, but also the thoracic and cervical joints. If your own favorite armchair is too deep, you can have a thick square-sided pillow to fill it in (Fig. 45).

(b) A Slanting Chair

Unless the back of the chair is long enough to support the head, it should not slant backward. If it does, and if it is not long enough to support the head, the buttocks begin to slide forward, the lumbar lordosis is lost, and the head, fighting against the pull of gravity, is forced forward into flexion, so that the cervical lordosis also disappears (Fig. 46). Not only the lower back but neck and shoulder areas also begin to ache. When visiting, you can perhaps make do by filling in with cushions, or you can turn sideways as mentioned before, using the chair arm as backrest, or ignore the backrest and lean forward using your muscles as on a backless seat. If your own chair is at fault, you should use a wedge-shaped back as for the car (see Chapter 8), or fill in with many cushions.

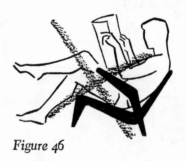

Figure 46

A SWIVEL CHAIR

This is designed for altering the height to suit the individual need but, unfortunately, it is usually constructed to swing back as well, so that it becomes the slanting chair discussed above, giving no support to the spine.

A LONG INCLINED CHAIR

Since the head can now be supported, this chair is both comfortable and safe, provided that the cervical and lumbar lordoses are filled in and the legs are not stretched forward without being bent, however little, at the knees (Fig. 47).

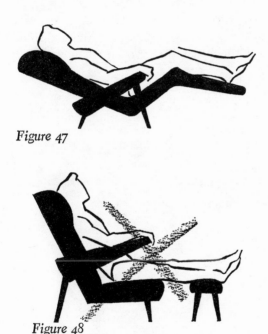

Figure 47

Figure 48

CHAIR AND STOOL COMBINATION

If sitting tends to open the lumbar joints posteriorly, this is even more true of sitting with the legs stretched forward at right angles to the body (the L-shaped position).

Luckily very few disc sufferers can stand this for long, and they are apt to think that by using a cushion in the lumbar spine all is well. The type of "father's chair" consisting of an armchair and footstool of the same height encourages this posture (Fig. 48), and is imitated when sitting on a sofa with the feet resting on a coffee table or the mantel-piece, a position favored by those who have been told to "keep their feet up" because of varicose veins.

A back sufferer must not sit with his feet up, as this is one of the positions which is likely to cause a disc lesion. You can have your feet up only when lying in the Supported Position, or with the legs bent and feet on the arm of a sofa (Fig. 49), or the legs on a slanting board with pillows under the knees (Fig. 50), or on a cushioned stool, or with the foot of the bed raised. An armchair with a low foot-

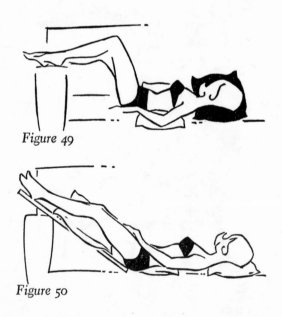

Figure 49

Figure 50

stool (Fig. 51), however, allows the legs to bend and is, on the other hand, a comfort to an aching back.

The "rule" for sitting is always the same: the knees must be allowed to bend.

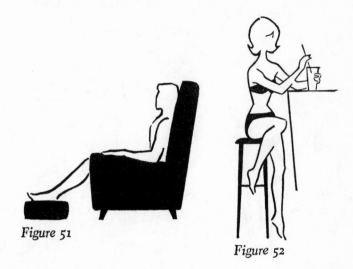

Figure 51

Figure 52

DECK CHAIRS

These have been discussed in "How to Lie." With a foot-rest they become too much like a "father's chair" unless the foot is half lowered.

HIGH SNACK BAR STOOLS

These are for the most part extremely uncomfortable as the feet cannot rest on the ground. If the bar itself has no overhang table top, there is no place for the knees as one leans over. It is best to sit on one buttock and reach one foot down to the ground as one would perch on a wall or veranda railing (Fig. 52).

RELATION OF CHAIR TO TABLE

Most chairs are too high in relation to the table, and when possible their legs should be cut shorter by two to four inches to avoid the sitter's stooping (Fig. 53).

When working you should pull the chair well under the table (impossible if the chair is too high) to avoid bending too far forward (Fig. 54).

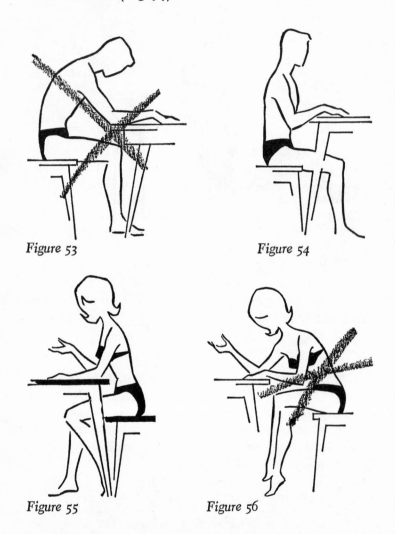

Figure 53

Figure 54

Figure 55

Figure 56

If possible the work, such as writing, should be done on a sloping surface, as on a draftsman's board.

If at table you find your chair is inadequate for leaning back, then forget Amy Vanderbilt and lean elbow or forearm on the table resting forward (Fig. 55).

This support becomes inadequate if you slump or cross the legs as the pull toward flexion is then increased (Fig. 56).

SITTING WITH LEGS CROSSED

Crossing the knees while sitting is not in itself harmful unless you feel an uncomfortable pull, but if this position is held for long it does tend to pull the buttocks away from the back support. It is useful when you write on your knee as it raises the level of the pad (Fig. 57).

Resting the side of the leg on the knee is sometimes more comfortable (Fig. 58).

Figure 57

Figure 58

SITTING UP IN BED

When you need to sit up in bed, make the pillows support the lumbar curve properly, and if your head is not also supported, sit upright. Be sure to bend or cross the legs, or to have a pillow under the knees to avoid the L-shaped position (Fig. 59).

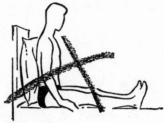

Figure 59

This position not only forces the lumbar joints open no matter how well supported they may be, but it also pulls on the dura mater via its continuation as the sciatic nerves. This may move the dura mater over the protruding disc fragment, sometimes causing increased pain, not necessarily at the time, and in the case of a slow protrusion perhaps not till next day.

If you must spend a long convalescence in bed and sit up for much of each day, you should have a proper backrest and knee rest for the bed.

SITTING ON THE GROUND

It is usually uncomfortable for a disc sufferer to sit on the ground. He can bend the knees and clasp them (Fig. 60), or bending one or both knees rest on the hands behind (Fig. 61).

If he sits cross-legged, he must hold onto the knees to prevent his sagging forward (Fig. 62).

Any of these postures is made comfortable by leaning against a wall or another's knee or back. He can also sit on his feet, Japanese fashion (Fig. 63).

Sitting with both legs on one side pulls the lumbar joints out of position (Fig. 64).

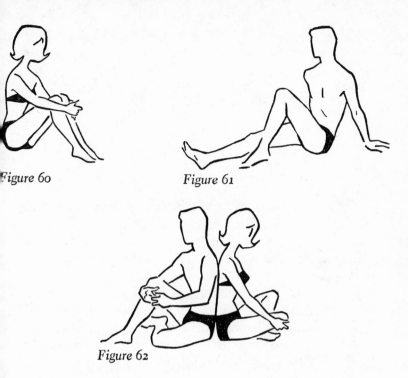

Figure 60

Figure 61

Figure 62

SITTING FOR LONG

Whenever you sit for very long, you need a support. A cushion is not always available, but on a journey, working, or in the theater, a folded raincoat, a sweater, a woman's handbag, or even a folded newspaper, etc., serves the purpose.

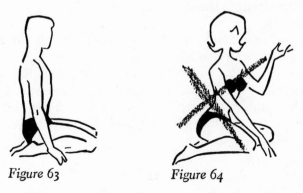

Figure 63

Figure 64

5: How to Stand and Walk

Since our forebears attained the erect position with much difficulty, we should endeavor to maintain it without damage to the intervertebral discs. We must therefore hold the body in the anatomical alignment so that (a) the weight of it does not damage the discs by uneven pressure at the circumference of the vertebral joints, and (b) these joints are not held for long out of the neutral position and thus allow a disc already cracked to protrude beyond the joint surfaces. To maintain the anatomical alignment of the body when standing one should:

1. *Lift the chest out of the abdomen.* This does not mean "hold the head up and pull the shoulders back" as some parents still instruct their children. No one can hold such a position for long without tiring. Lifting the chest out of the abdomen *automatically* puts the shoulders in a normal relaxed position, avoids "round shoulders," and brings the head up with chin parallel to the floor (Fig. 65).

2. *Think tall.* While keeping the head relaxed, think of yourself being suspended by a hair growing from the very top of the head. This prevents the muscles of the neck contracting more strongly in front or behind and keeps the chin parallel with the floor, and lessens the compression strain on the cervical joints supporting the weight of the head (Fig. 66).

Figure 65

Figure 66

3. *Contract the abdominal and gluteal muscles.* The *abdominal* muscles, consisting of four layers, each interwoven in a different direction, and attached to the ribs, the pelvis, and the fascia of the lower back, form a webbing over the abdomen which keeps the intestines from protruding forward in a "potbelly." If kept constantly tensed, they also prevent the lumbar curve from becoming exaggerated, i.e. they prevent the lumbar joints from opening too much anteriorly. They are apt to become infiltrated with fat, and together with the weight of the protruding intestines they pull the lumbar vertebrae down on one another. Persons with weak abdominal muscles are most liable to discopathy. Therefore these muscles must be strengthened. (See Chapter 9.)

Tensing the gluteal muscles balances the pull of the abdominal muscles, so that the lumbar curve is not allowed to disappear completely. Both groups working together form a natural girdle around the trunk; a girdle which, unless the body is lying down, should be constantly in slight tension underneath any other artificial girdle or belt. Since the position of the rest of the spine depends on lumbar posture, this is most important. It is the girdle

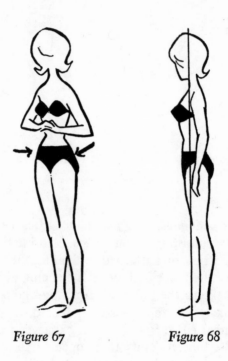

Figure 67   Figure 68

which maintains the young line of the body and avoids middle-age spread which in some individuals begins in childhood! When you become accustomed to the exercises in Chapter 9, it will be easy to hold the normal tension of your natural girdle (Fig. 67).

4. *Put the weight of the body forward on the balls of the feet, which should not be turned too far outward.* If the body is otherwise held correctly but the greater weight falls

on the heels, the compression strain will still be unevenly distributed on the joints of the spine. To judge your own standing position use this test: If without changing the body position you can lift the balls of the feet off the floor, you are not properly balanced, and the weight is certainly more on the heels. Sway slightly forward and you will find you cannot lift them; the heels now rest lightly on the floor because the weight is correctly distributed between ball of the foot and heel (Fig. 68).

If the feet are overeverted the ankle joint will feel an uncomfortable strain. Think of yourself as standing on the face of a clock about 2 feet in diameter with the feet slightly apart on either side of the center. They should point roughly at five minutes to one. If they exceed this and are nearer ten minutes to two, your feet are turned too far outward (Fig. 69).

Figure 69

The standing posture varies according to the need of the moment. The feet may be only slightly apart, which is most usual, or wide apart to give the body a larger standing base for more balance or rest as the "at ease" position of a soldier or that of someone on a heaving deck. One foot may be in front of the other, or the weight more on one foot than the other, or supported against a wall. All of these are correct so long as you remember to *lift the ribs out of the abdomen, stretch upward with the top of the head, contract the abdominal and gluteal muscles,* and to *keep the feet at the proper angle* so that the weight can fall forward on the balls of the feet.

WALKING

Walking is really progressing in a straight line while holding the body in the position just described, using the hips, knees, ankles, and toes as flexibly as possible, so that at each step the body is pushed forward by the toes and the head moves forward in a smooth line (Fig. 70). Because

Figure 70

of the forward push of the toes it is always easier and less tiring to stride along than to walk slowly with small steps.

For most people walking is merely a progression, full

stop. Watch people on the street. Some move as though their feet were strapped to pieces of board with practically no movement at ankles or toes. Others, usually the "pot-bellied" or those with weak abdominal muscles, hold the body tilted backward and come down heavily on their heels. These develop callosities, while the rubbers on the heels of their shoes are worn away at the back. Those with overeverted feet progress slowly or, if they try to hurry, heave the body from side to side so that the head bobs up and down. They wear their rubber heels away on the outside as well as at the back. Not only is it impossible to put the weight forward on the balls when the feet are turned outward, but since the toes are forced to bend upward as the body advances into the next step, each step becomes a progression not only forward but sideways (like a yacht tacking). This gait wastes a great deal more energy.

Watch a baby learning to walk. He will experiment with his feet wide apart for balance, but if you hold his attention by calling him to you he will lessen the evertion of his feet, push with his toes at each step to propel himself onward until he falls triumphant into your arms. Unfortunately, later on he forgets this great secret of the art of walking: toe work. Those who know how to walk come along at rarer intervals. They hold the body well, and go forward smoothly and apparently without effort. These people move like those you enjoy watching on stage or screen, like panthers or Greek athletes; they have beauty in movement. Once, in despair, I asked a patient who could not learn how to walk to go and see Sir Laurence Olivier in his next film. He came back later with a grin to tell me he had just been to see *Richard III!* If you have a mathematical brain perhaps you can work out how many steps you take a year. Don't pound your discs at each step. It is for you to decide whether your spine becomes gradually worse or better just by choosing the way you walk. If you have been walking incorrectly and now try the flexible way, expect foot and leg pains in the first few days. You are now using muscles you may never have used properly even as a child. It is appalling the number of children who stamp about on their heels like elephants. Unless shown something better, this becomes a habit which contributes toward future foot or spine trouble. Children are often given foot supports, when what they really need is to be shown how to use the muscles of the feet while walking.

HEIGHT OF HEEL

A heel helps to shift the weight of the body forward onto the ball, and this distributes the weight properly, as explained at the beginning of the chapter. For women the height of the heel on her shoe is an individual problem. Some people suffering from pressure on the sciatic nerve cannot and should not walk without a heel, since the stretch on the nerve is increased as the heel is lowered. Too high a heel throws too much weight onto the ball, pushes the toes against the front of the shoe, and overstrains the capsule and ligaments of the mid-tarsal joint. Were the heel support of shoes made to come further for-

Figure 71

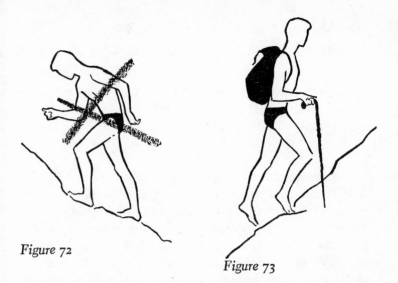

Figure 72

Figure 73

ward before sloping down, this would make them much
more comfortable. Indeed, modern Italian shoes show a
great improvement in shoe designing. Even for the same
person's foot the height of her heel can comfortably be
varied for different occasions. Use the heel which feels
right at the time.

WALKING UPSTAIRS OR UP A SLOPE

Walking upstairs you must keep the body upright and
place only the ball of the foot on each step (Fig. 71). You
will get up with far less effort. This is true also of going
uphill. A real mountaineer does not tire himself by bending
forward on a steep slope and putting his heel down (Fig.
72). The ankle and foot muscles are tremendously strong
and, if used properly, lift the body easily (Fig. 73).

6: How to Bend, Lift, and Carry

The spine is made up of joints so that we can move it. In view of the mechanics of the discs, it is unwise to force flexion of these joints too much, e.g. to bend down with straight legs to do something which can be done with less strain on spine and heart by squatting or kneeling. It will be seen that the classic exercise of gymnasts, for goodness knows how many years, of stretching to touch the toes or floor in whatever position, standing or lying, *is one which provokes disc displacement.* We do it because our fathers, grandfathers, and great-grandfathers have always done so. We learned it at school, and, *incredibly, this exercise is still being taught in schools.* It is supposed to be good for the abdominal muscles but done standing it merely relaxes them and returns them to their original position. Yet many a middle-aged person has first been made aware of the fact that he has a broken disc by bending to touch his toes as an exercise for reducing his "tummy," *which it cannot do.*

Trunk-flexing exercises could be said to be of some use to the back muscles, but these are far more adequately exerted in the acts of standing and walking, and they are strong muscles. In any case it is wrong to strain the spine, the human frailty, for the sake of these muscles, when there are other more effective exercises for this purpose.

You can force the spinal joints open at the back by lying, sitting, and standing incorrectly; more easily still if you bend wrongly. Unfortunately, at the time you do not always notice the effect, which would act as a warning. You may, of course, bend down to pick up something off the floor and feel a stab of pain in the back or the buttock, but you may also bend over for some time washing clothes or packing, and the ache may come on only some hours or days later, or another symptom of disc pressure, e.g. "nervous cystitis," or perhaps pains at the back of both legs may appear. In the first instance the protrusion is sudden, in the second it has oozed out more slowly, but in each case the joint has been opened unfavorably because you have neither bent the legs nor supported the body as gravity pulls the joint open (Fig. 74).

Figure 74

BEND THE LEGS

To bend down and pick up an object from the floor, bend the knees, and for greater comfort support the body by a hand on a chair, etc., or on the thigh itself (Fig. 75). If the knees are stiff or the muscles weak, raise one leg behind, pivoting on the other hip joint (Fig. 76). Again, placing a hand on a piece of furniture or the thigh helps.

To turn out a low drawer, to arrange records or books

on a low shelf, to plant seedlings, to change a tire, etc., get down to it. Don't stand with the buttocks in the air. You can squat, or kneel on one knee (Fig. 77), or both, or sit on your heels, or on a low box or stool (Fig. 78).

Do not, however, sit sideways on the floor as this opens the joints both laterally and posteriorly as you lean forward to work. To retrieve something which has fallen under a cupboard or sofa, go on all fours or lie flat (Fig. 79).

Figure 75

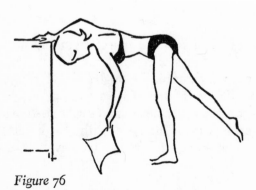

Figure 76

Figure 77

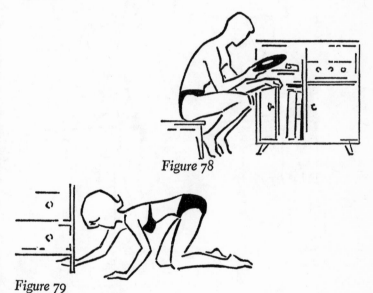

Figure 78

Figure 79

SUPPORT THE JOINT

When it feels easier to do so, lean on your hand, elbow, arm, knee, or leg to support the body against the pull of gravity. Rest a hand or knee on the side of the bathtub

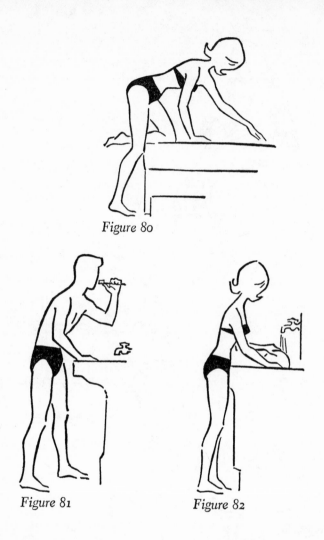

Figure 80

Figure 81   Figure 82

when turning on the taps, or on a bed to pick up something on the far side or to tuck in the sheets (Fig. 80).

Put a hand or forearm on the washbasin while brushing the teeth or washing the face. The wider the legs are apart, the further down you can get without flexing the trunk (Fig. 81).

When your disc lesion is active, bending forward only very slightly from the upright, as for instance while shaving or while washing dishes, may cause a twinge in the back. This is because the joint on first beginning to open posteriorly still supports the whole weight of the upper part of the body and compression then forces the disc further backward toward the dura mater. This can be greatly diminished by leaning the pelvis against the basin, or resting one foot on a stool to counteract the forward pull (Fig. 82). Rest a hand on a desk or table, etc., when talking to someone who is sitting (Fig. 83).

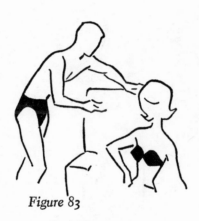

Figure 83

Brace one foot forward when pulling open a heavy door (Fig. 84).

Lean against the wall of the shower when washing your feet (Fig. 85), and support the arms on the wall or taps when letting the hot water flow over neck and back (Fig. 86).

Rest a hand on a chest of drawers to pull open a lower drawer (Fig. 87).

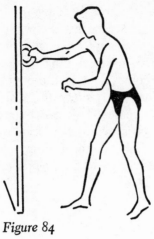

Figure 84

Figure 85

Figure 86

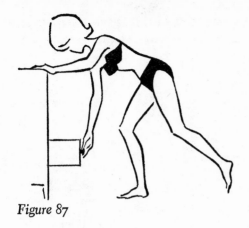

Figure 87

UNNECESSARY BENDING

There is often no need to bend down, for instance when passing a tray of drinks or food to someone seated, or when using a vacuum cleaner or broom (Fig. 88). When waxing the floor, to apply the wax use a mop or plastic squirter, but if you must do it by hand, kneel on a pad with the lumbar spine in lordosis (Fig. 89).

Figure 88

Figure 89

Do not work at a low table or sink when standing, as in carpentry or in a kitchen (Fig. 90). The table for standing work should be at least as high as the elbows (Fig. 91).

Figure 90   Figure 91

Expectant mothers should have a high table or chest of drawers ready for bathing the baby or changing its clothes.

You should not leave a suitcase on the floor and open it when you can just as well put it on the table, chest of drawers, or at least on the bed.

As coughing or sneezing compresses the spine it is unwise to bend forward while doing either; so try to put a steadying hand in the small of your back and remain upright, or better still bend slightly backward.

LIFTING

Lifting means bending with additional compression strain due to the weight to be lifted. It should be avoided when possible, and not attempted unless the knees are bent, and the body is as near as possible to the object, or supported. There should be no jerks. To lift a box, or a heavy

70

potted plant, put your feet on either side, bend the knees and then lift by straightening them (Fig. 92).

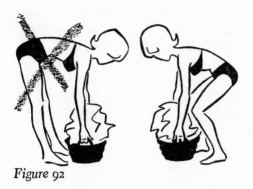

Figure 92

To lift a car hood or open the trunk, support the body with the other hand on the fender, or with the foot on the bumper.

To lift up the rolling door of a garage, put one foot a little in front of the other and support one hand on the thigh; this is a useful position also for lifting a heavy saucepan from a low kitchen shelf (Fig. 93).

Figure 93

When lifting a child, stand with legs wide apart before bending the knees, and if possible help him first onto a low stool or step. To lift a baby off a bed, rest a knee on the bed to take some of the weight, or if from a crib, rest the arms on the high sides.

Lifting a not too heavy armchair, rest it against the thigh or shin (Fig. 94), but a heavy overstuffed chair is better attempted with the help of someone else, each lifting an arm.

When moving a piece of furniture too heavy to lift, do not pull, but push, so that the lumbar lordosis is maintained (Fig. 95).

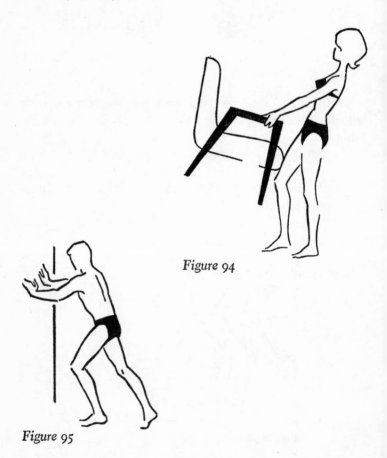

Figure 94

Figure 95

Figure 96

Figure 97

Pick up or put down a suitcase with one foot a little in front of the other, and bend the knees instead of bending over to one side (Figs. 96, 97).

Lifting must be done smoothly. If someone bends down to pull out a stump in the garden, he may be stuck in flexion by severe lumbago. Not only does the pull flex the joints more and increase the compression strain, but

Figure 98

Figure 99

Figure 100

the jerk exaggerates these two forces greatly. Moreover, the sudden movement of the stump coming out is in itself another jerk.

CARRYING

Keep the body as straight as possible, and divide the weight when practical, e.g. two medium-sized suitcases instead of one heavy one.

Figure 101

If a large one must be carried, do not let it pull you over but lean in the opposite direction (Fig. 98).

Let direct pressure on the pelvis relieve the spine of some of the weight whenever possible. Compression on the spine itself is diminished when carrying a small trunk against your pelvis (Fig. 99), a heavy parcel on your hip (Fig. 100), a child in front with the legs round your waist, on your hip, or piggyback (Fig. 101).

7: How to Look After Cervical and Upper Thoracic Disc Lesions

The abdominal and gluteal muscles can be trained to protect the lumbar spine, but the cervical spine is not so well organized. Its greater mobility makes it more difficult for a patient with a chronic cervical disc lesion, once reduced, to keep the fragment of disc in place unless he does the exercises of Chapter 9. Maintain the normal relaxed anatomical position of the head and neck, remembering that the neck movements affect the upper part of the thoracic spine too. The Corrective Movements for the cervical region have been described (rhythmic movements in all directions to centralize the discs) but to *remain* in any one extreme position for long forces the cervical and upper thoracic joints out of alignment and provokes a disc protrusion. This may cause, perhaps, not only pain in the muscles of or near the neck, but may spread to one or both shoulders or arms. It may cause pain behind or in front of the chest, including "fibrositis" or "trigger points." Sometimes there is headache, or "migraine," dizziness and humming in the ears often mistaken for "labyrinthitis," numbness or pins and needles in one or both arms or hands or feet. These symptoms naturally do not all come at once but the patient may suffer from one or more of them. Here then are some of the positions which cause cervical disc lesions, and which should not be maintained for any length of time:

This position is held when one looks up at a plane, or talks to someone who is above at an upstairs window or on a deck of a ship (Fig. 102).

A habit picked up in childhood, by one small for his age or determined not to be shy, is to walk with the chin held above the normal level like "little Johnny-head-in-air" (Fig. 103).

Figure 102

Figure 103

At the hairdresser a woman sometimes has difficulty when the attendant wants to force her head backward over the basin for washing her hair (Fig. 104). She should ask that the adaptable basin be raised to her requirement. (Should she have to slide down in the chair because the basin cannot be made higher, she should protect her lumbar lordosis with her "girdle" muscles.)

The movie theater presents a problem with its high screen, as even in the back seats you have usually to raise the head above normal. This posture is exaggerated if you have to sit near the front.

Figure 104

FLEXION

This position is that most commonly held, unintentionally, when you sit to read. Bring the book or paper up to eye focus. Do not read with the book on your lap (Fig. 105). Rest the elbows, or at least one, on the armrests of the chair (Fig. 106). If there is no armrest, cup the elbow in the other hand (Fig. 107) or cross one knee over the other and rest the book on this. A pillow will raise the book still higher (Fig. 108).

For hand sewing also make use of the arm or knee rest with pillow, or if there is much work to spread out, sit up to a table and lean both elbows on it to bring the work up to eye focus (Fig. 109).

Figure 105

Figure 106

Machine sewing is rather trying if you use a treadle as it is difficult to get near enough to the work. Even if you have an electric machine, your chair must be low enough to prevent your bending forward.

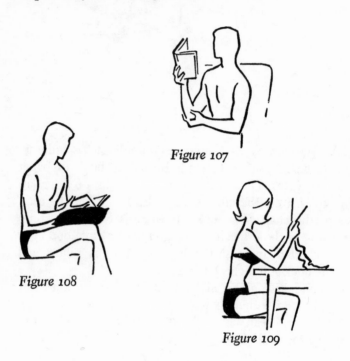

Figure 107

Figure 108

Figure 109

The same applies to writing, and you should not work for too long a time. Typewriters are constructed on an inclined plane to enable the user to sit upright and you should copy this admirable arrangement when writing by hand. All you need is a firm background for your writing material, such as a hard blotter or a piece of compressed cardboard, which can be supported on a couple of books to give it the required tilt. If you have to write much, you should have a light wooden inclined wedge made, measuring about 12 by 10 inches and with a height of 6 inches,

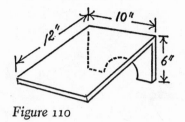

Figure 110

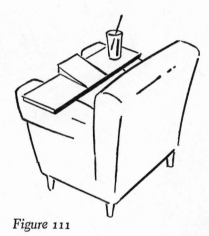

Figure 111

covered with blotting paper or felt (Fig. 110). This can be used on a table, or on a pillow on the knee when you write sitting in an armchair (Fig. 111).

Propping up the chin with one hand while writing at a table is helpful (Fig. 112), or with both hands while thinking about what one is going to write (Fig. 113).

If you work standing at a table, it should be at least as high as the level of the elbows; raise it on blocks if it is not.

Avoid the inclined chair or car seat which forces the head forward in self-defense against the pull of gravity.

Figure 112

Figure 113

Figure 114

On a journey long enough to make you sleepy, be sure the neck is properly supported and that your head does not fall forward on the chest (Fig. 114).

When washing the hair at home, a woman should go under the shower to avoid bending low over a handbasin. At the hairdresser's when the drier is applied, she should stretch up to her full height while it is adjusted, or she will find that her head has been forced into flexion.

Walking looking at the ground is another habit acquired in childhood through shyness (Fig. 115). This is easily corrected once the victim knows about it. When you sleep on your side do not bend the chin onto the chest. Reading while lying on the back with too low a pillow forces the neck forward to read (Fig. 116). While reading do not rest the head on the back of the bed.

Figure 115

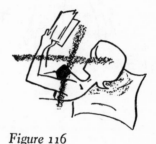

Figure 116

ROTATION

The neck is forced into rotation to allow for breathing when you sleep on the front. This is a habit hard to break, but the pillow under the knee in side-lying helps to wake you if you turn over onto your front. Sleeping thus is a very common cause of a cervical disc lesion, and if you already have trouble will always tend to make this worse.

Avoid a seat at the side of the movie theater, as this means your neck is twisted to one side as well as being extended to see the screen. When sitting on a sofa talking to someone at your side, instead of keeping the head twisted, turn around to face him, using the armrest as a back support (Fig. 117).

When typing from copy be sure this is propped up in

Figure 117

Figure 118

Figure 119

front of your typewriter and not flat on the table at the side (Fig. 118).

Dancing cheek to cheek is also uncomfortable for a

woman with a cervical or thoracic disc lesion, but there are compensations!

Arrange your chair to face T.V. comfortably (Fig. 119).

SIDE FLEXION

As you lie on your side in bed, check your posture in a mirror to be sure that the neck is not being pushed out of alignment to one side or the other. A sagging bed leaves the neck flexed to the side away from the pillow, since the head, not being as heavy as the trunk, does not also sag (Fig. 120). This bad position is imitated when, while lying on your side, you prop the head up by the hand (Fig. 121).

Holding the head to one side is also a habit acquired in childhood.

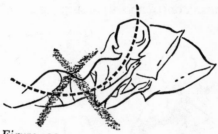

Figure 120

Figure 121

Sitting behind someone tall in the theater makes you flex to the side to look around him. As any position in the theater is held for at least two hours, it is a good thing to move the head occasionally during the show and afterward make a point of doing the Corrective Movements as soon as you can; this avoids ill-effects the day after.

BRUSQUE ARM MOVEMENTS

Because of the way the muscles are arranged, movements of the arms affect the neck and upper thoracic joints. Care must therefore be taken to avoid certain brusque movements. They are, for instance, beating eggs or cake mixtures vigorously (Fig. 122). A rotary beater can be used for eggs, and if you have no electric beater you can stir your cake mixture slowly.

A dog who pulls hard on the leash may upset a sensitive neck (Fig. 123); so may energetic shaking of a cocktail mixer or strenuous polishing of a car or furniture.

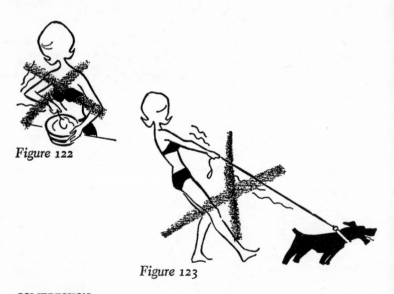

Figure 122

Figure 123

COMPRESSION

Since the joints at the top of the spine are small and comparatively fragile, even moderate compression may increase disc trouble. Talking vigorously with the head is rather like hitting a wooden hammer on half a dozen prune stones piled one on top of another. Learn to use the head smoothly and, if you must gesticulate, use your hands.

Lifting the head while lying causes much compression at the upper joints. When lying prone you should support the head either by crossing the hands under the chin, or by cupping it in them (Figs. 124, 125). Lying supine, support the neck with the hands when you lift your head or raise the upper half of the body with elbows or hands (Fig. 126). However, none of these positions—even though supported—should be held for long.

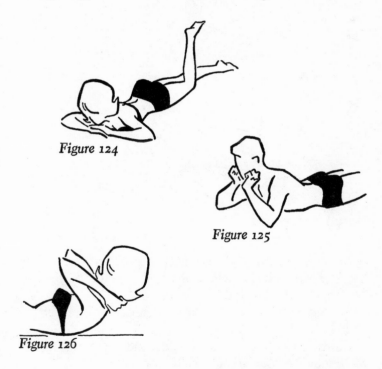

Figure 124

Figure 125

Figure 126

Diving headfirst is strongly compressive, as is also the pounding of a large wave on your head, or diving through it, or a child in the water pulling on your head (Fig. 127). A woman will lose the benefit of floating the head if she is vigorously contracting the neck muscles to keep her hair from getting wet (Fig. 128). Be careful not to pull on a bathing cap too vigorously.

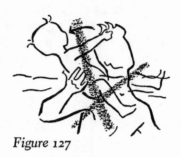

Figure 127

Figure 128

At the hairdresser's do not let the assistant wash or dry the hair with much friction; if she does, steady the head by cupping the chin with the hands.

Beware of pressing the head up against the head of the bed.

Knitting for long tenses the arms and the neck muscles and should be done in short spells only.

Carrying heavy packages or the heavy load of small pieces of luggage will pull unfavorably on the neck, as will the daily use of a heavy handbag or brief case, as often as not filled with unnecessary objects (Fig. 129).

Figure 129

Unpleasant emotions such as anger, fear, or business tension will contract the muscles and pull the joints closer together. This is how some nervous tension headaches arise, and a broken disc in the cervical area increases this tendency.

To relieve compression strain you must carry out the Corrective Movements with the head in the hands, lifting the weight off the joints as explained at the end of Chapter 2.

8: How to Avoid
Increased Compression Strain

Man's spine is inadequate for the stresses and strains of modern life. If he is to continue without increasing disc trouble, he must go back to the four-paw position or swing from trees, or learn to live on two legs avoiding increased compression strain. The latter is by far the most practical! True, some people do exercise on all fours, but it is doubtful whether the short time spent in this position is of much help. Others enjoy hanging from a door or a bar at home, but again this cannot be done for long and the effect is canceled if one jumps down to the floor afterward. Both cause discomfort when a cervical or upper thoracic lesion is present. In any case, these positions benefit only lumbar and lower thoracic disc lesions. Let us see how to diminish compression strain throughout the twenty-four hours of the day.

1. *First learn to hold the spine in the position which does not exert 'undue compression on any part of the joint.*

This is the posture that maintains the cervical and lumbar curves. Lift the chest out of the abdomen, contract the abdominal and gluteal muscles slightly, and put the weight forward on the balls of the feet like a man about to dive. Think tall as though you were suspended to the ceiling by a long hair growing out of the top of your head, keeping the shoulders and neck relaxed (Fig. 130). When sitting you must maintain this position, keeping the buttocks well against the back of the seat and keeping the spine *vertical* by adequate back support. At the same time aim at keeping the abdominal and gluteal muscles slightly contracted. This amounts to a minor form of yoga (Fig. 131). Each time you find you are slumped forward with tiredness, gently correct your position (Fig. 132). After a while you will find it actually relieves your weariness. Exercises for strengthening these muscles you will find in Chapter 9.

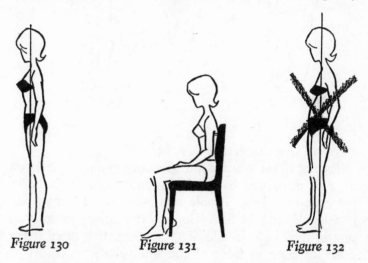

Figure 130   Figure 131   Figure 132

2. Avoid Overweight ·

Much weight put on steadily and rapidly often heralds the beginning of disc trouble; and if someone has been suffering only slightly, the condition may suddenly become worse. Yet adults will gain from five to ten pounds a year without realizing it until faced with the problem of reducing fifty pounds (Fig. 133). It is as though they were carrying a heavy sackload hung from the shoulders (Fig. 134). The muscles attached to the spine, loaded with fat, and the large abdomen continually engorged, pull the joints closer together. Any overweight person suffering from disc trouble should reduce to his normal weight if he is to avoid further attacks.

Figure 133

Figure 134

3. *Avoid Carrying Heavy Weights*

Try not to carry heavy suitcases or shopping bags. If you have to, distribute the weight on both sides. Avoid heavy objects on the head. People who have carried heavy loads from childhood have developed extra strong muscles to protect the joints. In addition, the spine itself often forms beaks of bone in front of the weak joints which act as individual corsets to these joints. Until recently this form of calcification was regarded in medicine as a disease. Now it is recognized as a defense mechanism of the spine, without which manual laborers would have to give up their jobs at a much earlier age, and old people, nearly all of whom have cracked discs, would be bedridden with pain (Fig. 9, Chap. 2).

4. *Wear a Belt*

Women are much less muscular than men and are more comfortable and much safer using an elastic girdle. This serves two purposes—it acts like a second skin, giving a feeling of support, and it reminds the wearer to train the *muscular* girdle underneath. She must not rely on the belt then as her sole support. A man with exceptionally flabby girdle muscles, a long weak back, or a feeling of great insecurity may need a sports belt at least for a while until he can get back into condition. Often the flabbiness is caused by *the pressure of the disc on the roots of the nerves supplying these muscles* and they are suffering from mild paralysis. Later when the displacement of the disc is reduced they are much easier to control. When one is treated with the latest Cyriax methods it is seldom that an orthopedic corset is necessary. Many a sufferer who has had to wear one has been happy to take it off once the displacement of the disc has been reduced.

5. *Avoid Jumping and Slipping*

When getting down from a stool or a ladder, step down smoothly, and when having to jump from a bank or a wall use a helping hand or a branch, and land with bended knees on the balls of the feet. Be careful of slipping on wet pavements or walking into the unmended holes in road or pavement.

6. *Avoid Running*

Do not run for exercise, though if you are playing a game or running to catch a bus this is only a small sprint and should be done on the balls of the feet, not on the heels.

7. *Avoid Sitting Down Heavily*

Sitting down and getting up should be graceful movements. Many people, instead of sitting down throw themselves into a seat with a jarring motion. Think how many times a year you repeat this action and calculate the wear and tear on the spine. The best way to cure this habit is to stand in front of a chair in view of a mirror at the side. Put one foot slightly in front of the other to keep a good balance, and with a straight spine sit down and get up without using the hands, ten times. This may prove more difficult than you expect at the beginning as it requires much coordination of trunk and leg muscles, but once you have acquired the technique, it will solve the problem. A low seat is more difficult to lower yourself into, and a hand on the arm of the chair is a help.

8. *Avoid Walking Heavily on the Heels*

If this is one of your habits, and you can tell by looking to see if the heels of your shoes are worn, remember how many steps you take in the course of a year and study again Chapter 5.

9. *Avoid Brusque and Very Rigorous Dancing*

Normal ballroom dancing with the weight on the balls of the feet is a smooth and *rhythmic* movement good for the spine, but dancing heavily on the heels or stamping jar it. You must know *how* to do a Scottish reel, a Czardas, or a Spanish dance. Watching a dancer like Antonio of Spain, one sees absolute control of the spine by superb muscle work when the heels hammer down. Incidentally, ballet begun in early years also develops muscle control. Even work at the "barre" involves only trunk flexion over *one* leg, which does not pull the lumbar joints open.

10. *Avoid Diving*

Diving from the diving board or the edge of the pool causes an impact of head or feet on the water which strongly compresses the spine (Fig. 135). In the sea and on a rough day don't penetrate the big breakers head on, or let large waves pound down on the head and shoulders. Ride over them or dive under as they approach until you are beyond them in smooth water.

11. *Be Careful About Games and Gymnastics*

A strong athlete or one who uses well-developed muscles constantly in his work has a natural protection for his spine. Should he by misfortune slip a disc while running, jumping, or twisting, with early and proper treatment he does not have to abandon sport but can carry on almost immediately. It is a joy to deal with him and see the rapid improvement and the little treatment needed. A less fit person often takes much longer to recuperate and should first learn abdominal and gluteal control before returning to sport or gymnastics (Chapter 9).

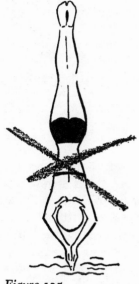

Figure 135

Golf will certainly be possible for nearly everyone unless he has a severe low thoracic disc lesion, which is the occupational disease of the professional golfer. A good follow-through is not a brusque movement, though digging up the turf is. Walking done properly is splendid. Tennis, because of its abrupt runs and stops, smashing serves and lunges will be more difficult. Riding is good if you know how to move with the horse. A good horseman sits erect and uses his girdle muscles quite strongly. All the stretching-up games such as netball are possible if you run and jump correctly. Fencing and skiing need and build good muscles. All sports have their pros and cons.

After disc trouble first learn how to defend your spine in standing; and then see what you can do!

The only sport *ideal* for the spine is swimming, but once again, not diving (Fig. 136). If you could stay in or under the water for the rest of your life like a fish, there would be no more disc trouble for you. Some patients complain that even swimming hurts, but so does practically every-

Figure 136

thing until a large protrusion has been reduced. Any stroke which feels good is good, and merely floating in the water is of benefit, and all the pillows of the sea are at your disposal. Here is your perfect mattress!

In gymnastics avoid going back to any of the idiotic flexion exercises, i.e. trying to reach the floor or the toes (Figs. 137, 138), and to vigorous jumping exercises. Concentrate more on those which stretch and extend the spinal joints.

12. *Avoid Overcontraction of the Trunk Muscles*

When the muscles of the trunk go into strong contraction, the joints are also brought nearer together. Be care-

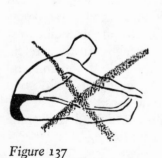

Figure 137

Figure 138

ful then of intense cold; going into cold water when the muscles are already trembling with cold is quite different from finishing off a hot shower with a cold one. Don't get into a freezing bed. In any case you will relax more quickly and sleep better lying first in warm sheets. Avoid sitting or lying in a draught, for you may "catch a cold in the neck." This sort of stiff neck cannot happen to someone with all his cervical discs intact.

Pain will also cause overcontraction of these muscles and is one of the contributing causes of disc trouble after painful childbirth. Many patients who have a troublesome cervical disc find they cannot stand painful "reducing" massage while lying prone: a combination of contracted muscles and unfortunate joint position. When lying prone or supine, do not lift up the head and remain in this position without support, for this posture involves contraction of the muscles around the neck (Figs. 139, 140).

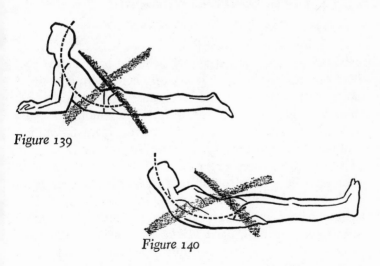

Figure 139

Figure 140

Coughing and sneezing are strong contractors of the trunk muscles. Patients who after treatment may have gone without further trouble for years may find that their symptoms sometimes return after a bad cold with cough. Avoid bending forward while coughing and sneezing (Fig. 141). If you can stay in bed during this phase of a cold, so much the better.

Figure 141

Emotion also plays a part in contracting the trunk muscles. Rage, shock, fear, and misery all affect disc trouble.

13. *Defend Your Spine During Transport*

Car Seat

In all forms of transport there is vibration, i.e. additional persistent compression strain. Where the back of the seat is of normal height, as in a car, or where there is none at all as on a motor bike, the body must be held upright. A man who has his own car is fortunate, more so if he drives, because he is in front where there is least vibration and he holds onto the steering wheel for further steadiness. However, this advantage is canceled if he sits with his spine rounded where there should be a lumbar lordosis, or leans back on a slanting seat with his head bent forward to counteract the pull of gravity or to see better (Fig. 142). *The joints are now open at the back while being compressed.* To avoid this he must push his buttocks back firmly. If the seat has an almost vertical back, he will need only a pillow about a foot square from the hollow of the back upward. If he has a gadget for altering the angle of the seat, this should be set at the most upright position. Moving the seat nearer to or further from the steering wheel has nothing to do with the problem. This does not alter the slant of the back of the seat.

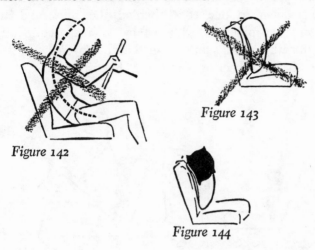

Figure 142

Figure 143

Figure 144

The American type of car seat is usually very slanting. It is sometimes possible to have a heel of wood or metal put under the front seat to tilt it forward and decrease the incline. The usual wicker or nylon back support by itself is useless. Though it supports the lumbar curve, it bends backward at the top like the car seat, exaggerating the total incline of the seat (Fig. 143). You will need a pillow tied onto the top to fill the gap and to continue the straight line, increasing the height so that there is adequate support across the shoulder blades (Fig. 144). Otherwise the lumbar spine will improve to the detriment of the neck and scapular areas, and they instead will begin to tire or ache after driving. An alternative is a wedge-shaped foam rubber pillow (sold as a seat pillow), thick enough at the top to fill the gap behind the shoulders and tapering down to nothing *just above* the buttocks. This wedge needs to be attached to the back of the seat to prevent its slipping down too low. Even so it will only help if the buttocks are pressed against the back of the seat.

A simpler homemade wedge can be constructed by making one pillow roughly 18 by 15 inches and shaking the stuffing down to one edge. Behind the thick end attach another pillow roughly 15 by 12 inches and sew them together. This support can then be covered and suspended from the back of the car seat (Fig. 145).

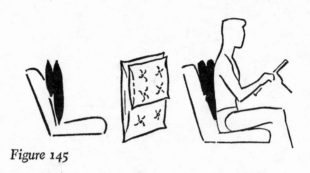

Figure 145

On a rough road beware of ruts and holes. If they damage the shock absorbers of your car, what do you think they do to the shock absorbers of your spine? If you cannot avoid them, pull in strongly your abdominal and gluteal muscles.

In a taxi, bus, or train, you can lean slightly forward to hold onto the seat in front or more comfortably with one elbow push the upper part of the back forward to keep the spine vertical for a short while (Fig. 146). On a longer journey make shift with a folded raincoat behind your back or anything else practical. The last few seats of a bus should be avoided as the vibration is greater. When standing in a bus it is often necessary to raise the heels slightly to prevent jarring.

Figure 146

A truck or Jeep has much more vibration, but in compensation has generally fairly upright seats. In these vehicles you should have a foam rubber pad on which to sit.

In a train, plane, and motor coach you have the advantage of a tall seat so that the cervical lordosis can be protected as well (Fig. 147). Hence you can recline. If there is a gap in the lumbar curve fill with a sweater, etc. Even in a motor coach do not sit in the last few seats. A jet plane may not vibrate in flight but does so on the ground and during takeoff, when you should contract your abdomen and buttocks.

Figure 147

You do not usually feel the effect of vibration at the time unless a disc lesion is very troublesome, but if the Corrective Movements are not done at the end of the journey or at the end of the day, the disc may continue slowly to move, and pain is felt perhaps two or three days afterward, when the journey has been forgotten. However, most disc sufferers are very weary after a long journey. This weariness is the forerunner of pain, and a warning sign. It means—take a hot shower or bath to relax the muscles, do your Corrective Movements to start the disc back on its inward journey, and with a hot cup of tea or a relaxing drink, lie down in the Supported Position. After ten to fifteen minutes you are once more ready for a full evening, which beforehand seemed quite impossible.

A bicycle is no problem unless the seat is high as in a racing model. A motor bike makes for a very good position. A horse, mule, or donkey needs extra control, but a camel would no doubt be a real problem! A ship, with its steady vibration for days on end, is very trying to most patients with a chronic cervical disc lesion. One must try to keep away from the more intensely vibrating points of the ship, and remember to protect the curves especially while in a deck chair. Deck games, dancing, and the swimming pool help to diminish the vibration.

14. *Lie Down During the Day*

If you have one or more broken discs in the spine which give trouble at times, you should form a habit of lying down at least once during the day and for at least ten minutes. In standing the spine bears the weight from the top of the head to the sacrum, and therefore all discs are under compression. During sitting this strain is present too (Fig. 148). For the legs it is a welcome relief, giving an illusion that the whole body is rested. But the sitting position, even when as favorable as possible, pulls the lumbar joints slightly open at the back so that if a disc is pressing on the dura mater quite strongly, the patient is in increased pain when he sits, or, having sat for some time,

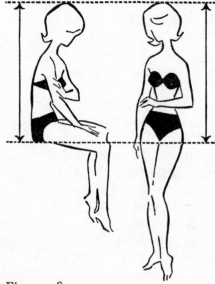

Figure 148

he cannot get up without difficulty because compression has squeezed the disc still further backward. Only by lying, therefore, is compression diminished. Most people are out of bed more than twelve hours a day, and many eighteen hours or more; this is too much for someone with disc trouble. A usually convenient time to lie down is after lunch, or just before, while waiting for the meal. If this is impossible for you, try resting when you come in from shopping or from business, before dinner. The best way to lie is on the back in the Supported Position and you should do your Corrective Movements first to get the full benefit from your short rest. When your disc lesion is particularly troublesome, try to lie down as often as possible during the day in ten-minute spells.

9: Exercises for the Spine

To hold the intervertebral discs inside the joints of the spine one must have strong trunk muscles, especially those of the lower trunk. To strengthen and maintain muscle tone, muscles should be contracted in two ways, ISO-TONICALLY and ISOMETRICALLY.

ISOTONIC contractions are those done repeatedly, and with some movement. ISOMETRIC contractions are those done with one long contraction and no movement.

The exercises must be done on a bed or couch, LYING IN THE SUPPORTED POSITION (Fig. 149), if the discs are not to be forced out of place. They should not be done on the floor. You should do the exercises *daily*, so that no strain during sport is put directly on the unprotected joints. Most people play golf or tennis, etc., only at the weekends, leaving the muscles to degenerate for the other five days. No wonder they sometimes develop a "muscle sprain" in the trunk during play. There is nothing wrong with the muscle; it has merely contracted to support the protruding disc from further damage.

It is important not to become breathless or to hold the breath during the exercises. You should breathe deeply when necessary. The lungs are like sacks, and to fill them one must open the nostrils and let the air fall in, expanding the lower part of the ribs, while the shoulders remain relaxed (Fig. 150). When the lungs are full, let the air flow out, contracting the abdomen slightly to force out the residue (Fig. 151). Deep breathing helps relaxation and di-

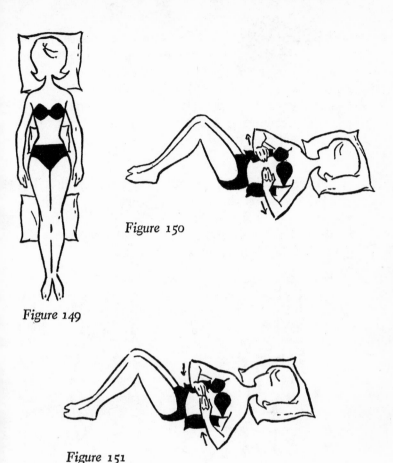

Figure 150

Figure 149

Figure 151

minishes pain. You should practice it when in much pain.

Exercises and breathing are done to a count of 1 *and* 2 *and* 3 *and* 4. I have suggested where breathing may be inserted. The contractions should be done as strongly as possible until the muscles tremble. Please read all the chapter before attempting the exercises.

1. With legs straight, and R foot crossed over L (a) try to pull feet apart (legs are still crossed) as hard as you can 4 times (Isotomic). Then pull apart once while counting 1 to 4 (Isometric). (b) Force R foot down, and L foot up against R 4 times (feet are still crossed). Repeat while counting up to 4. Breathe in for 4 and out for 4. Cross L foot over R and repeat (a) and (b).

2. With legs straight and parallel, alternately pull R hip upward toward R shoulder, and L hip up to L shoulder, and at the same time stretch other leg down toward the foot of the bed 4 times. Hold for 4. (Fig. 152.) Begin with L hip and repeat. Breathe 4 + 4.

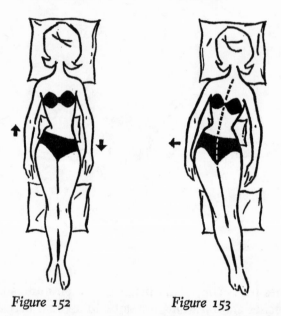

Figure 152   Figure 153

* 3. Push alternately R hip as far as possible to R and then L hip to L 4 times. Hold 4. (Fig. 153.) Begin with L hip and repeat. Breathe 4 + 4.

*4. Pull in muscles of the abdomen, buttocks, and the pelvic floor, i.e. anus (and vagina) 4 times (Fig. 154). Hold 4. Repeat. You can vary this by pulling in the abdominal muscles and the buttocks alternately. If the abdominals are very weak it may be easier to do the exercise with the knees together and bent so that the feet rest on the bed (Fig. 155).

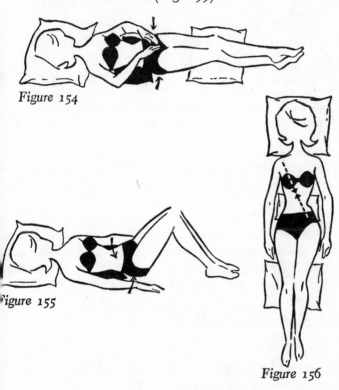

Figure 154

Figure 155

Figure 156

*5. With buttocks in contact with the bed, alternately pull the R hip inward and across toward L shoulder, then the L hip inward and across to R shoulder, 4 times. Hold 4. (Fig. 156.) Begin with L hip and repeat. Breathe 4 + 4.

*6. With hands at sides, lift both legs keeping them straight, not more than 12 inches off the bed and hold for 4. (Do not lift 4 times.) (Isometric.) (Fig. 157.) Repeat. Breathe 4 + 4.

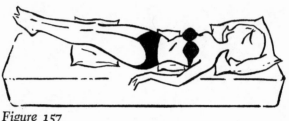

Figure 157

*7. With neck and buttocks in contact with the bed, arch the spine away from bed 4 times. Hold 4. Repeat.

Exercises 8–12 are for the upper half of the trunk, but anyone suffering from a cervical or thoracic disc lesion needs strong lower trunk muscles to hold steady the base of the spine. Conversely, if you have a lumbar disc lesion, you are liable to a cervical or thoracic disc lesion if you do not strengthen the muscles of the upper trunk.

8. With arms outstretched at shoulder level and elbows bent to 90 degrees (Fig. 158):
    (a) Hold fingers pointing to ceiling, force the elbows down against bed 4 times. Force down and hold for 4.
    (b) Resting forearms in front on bed, press down 4 times. Hold 4.
    (c) Resting forearms backward on bed, press down 4 times. Hold 4. Breathe 4 + 4.

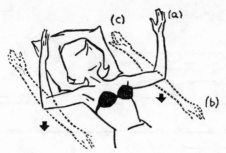

Figure 158

9. (a) Hold each arm just above elbow, and try to pull arms apart 4 times. Hold 4.

(b) Press arms together 4 times. Hold 4.

Repeat a and b holding wrists instead of arms. Breathe 4 + 4.

* 10. Make sure the nape of the neck is fully supported.

(a) Without bending the neck, press the head down and back on bed 4 times. Hold for 4.

(b) With fists pressing against underside of chin, press head forward and down on chest 4 times. Hold for 4.

(c) With R palm pressing against R cheek *turn* head to R 4 times. Hold for 4. Repeat to L.

(d) With R palm against R ear *bend* head to R 4 times. Hold for 4. Repeat to L. Breathe 4 + 4.

* 11. With elbows at sides, and head held in alignment with trunk, lift upper part of the body once off bed, not more than 12 inches, and hold for 4 (Fig. 159). Head must not be bent forward. (Isometric.)

Figure 159

* 12. Repeat Exercise No. 7.

13. Bend knees up to chest (Fig. 160). Straighten legs and keeping knees straight, spread and shut 4 times (Fig. 161). Hold open for 4. Repeat. Bend knees and return to start. Breathe 4 + 4.

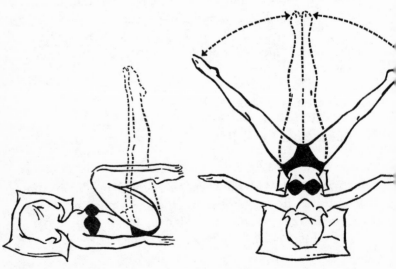

Figure 160   *Figure 161*

14. Take away knee pillow and lumbar pillow and lie on R side:

    (a) Raise L leg 4 times. Raise and hold 4.

    (b) Raise L leg as high as possible and swing forward and backward 4 times. Breathe 4 + 4. (Fig. 162.)

Lie on L side and repeat with R leg.

Figure 162

15. Lie on front. Lift R leg up and behind as far as possible 4 times. Lift and hold 4. Repeat with L leg. Breathe 4 + 4.

16. Repeat Exercise No. 7.

Exercise No. 4 can be repeated sitting, and all day long, e.g. while waiting in the car. The abdominal muscles are the most important of all to re-educate. People with weak abdominal muscles have more disc trouble than others. If you feel you need more exercise, repeat the three groups twice, or increase the count to 8 for each exercise. Do not overdo them at first. It is much more important to do the exercises conscientiously once every day than to skip some days and then do many.

Do the Corrective Movements of Chapter 2 before and after the Exercises.

There is no need to do all the exercises at once. You can for instance do 1–12 in the morning in bed, and 13–16 before your rest after lunch or at night.

When you have become accustomed to the exercises you will find it natural to stand and sit with the abdominal and gluteal muscles pulled in.

If you do not like to do exercises (and you have my sympathy), but need to re-educate the weak muscles, try at least to do the essential numbers marked * or begin with these.

Once learned, these exercises can be done in five to ten minutes. If you like doing exercises, and can do all these sixteen without strain, you can progress to any others you like, so long as you avoid those which flex the body unduly, as in straight leg toe touching, or those which continue to increase your pain after the first two or three days.

10: Why So Much Disc Trouble?

According to a recent German medical report, between 80 and 90 percent of all adults suffer at some time or other from a disc lesion. This is no exaggeration. But why? Most animals stand on all fours, so that the spinal column lies horizontally. With any increase of weight the spine sags downward, closing the joints posteriorly and opening them in front. Should a disc become cracked the possible protrusion is therefore harmlessly forward, away from the spinal canal.

Man, on the other hand, has by his superior intelligence learned to stand on two legs. Unfortunately, this means that the alignment of the vertebrae is now changed from horizontal to vertical, the weight of each pressing on top of the other, with the additional mass of the head forming a heavy load.

This then is the heritage of man's achievement of the erect position—compression strain.

The discs can now slip forward *or* backward and, as most of his movements are forward in flexion, the protrusion is very often backward when the joint opens posteriorly.

The discs most frequently broken are those at the bottom of the load, between the last lumbar vertebrae and the sacrum. In the cervical spine the lower discs are also most often broken. Those of the thoracic spine are more protected by the attachment of the ribs to the sternum, both of which tend to limit movement. Animals like bears can stand on their hind legs, but spend most of their time on four paws. Monkeys spend much of their time swinging from bough to bough so that compression strain is compensated. Scientists say that the modification by evolution of man's spine is not yet complete. Anyone looking down from about ten stories at people immediately below may verify this. About 35 percent of them appear to be going to fall flat on their faces. Fifty percent seem to be progressing only with the greatest difficulty and may fall any minute on the backs of their heads. The other 15 percent move well, seen even from that peculiar angle. Having attained the erect position, man must have managed quite well at first. He was heavily muscled and probably extremely strong for his size. To exist at all he had to defend himself from many larger animals with a club or a primitive stone ax or spear, and only the fittest survived. He also had to work hard to feed himself. He hunted other animals, went in search of roots, leaves, and berries, and his food, when he found it, was complete and gave him all that he needed for strength. To cover long distances in search for food he had to walk, and when he discovered how to ride he developed still stronger muscles to stay on the back of an animal with neither saddle nor bridle.

Nowadays his descendant by and large does not rely on his muscles for survival. He no longer defends himself against wild beasts. The competition is quite different. He sits behind a desk for at least five days of the week using not his muscles but his brains. Then, because his body cries out for some sort of normal activity, he spends—unless too exhausted by his unnatural life—one or two days at some sport. This means that flabby muscles are suddenly called upon for unusual effort for which they are often unprepared, and the strain falls on the joints instead.

Having earned his living by sitting all day, what foods does he buy himself? Certainly not those to give him strength and energy and build strong muscles, ligaments, and resistant cartilage to last more than twenty to thirty years. The foods and drinks which he chooses are for the most part made of refined sugars and starches, which tend to make him obese. He also eats too much because these foods do not satisfy him. They are grown or grazed on land deprived of much of its wealth as a result of deforestation. Once collected, these foods lose further mineral and vitamin value either by being refined, or by delay before they are actually eaten. Some of these lost minerals and vitamins, when the lack in the body has become very marked, can be replaced by buying them at great expense from a druggist, but they are not the perfectly balanced complete supply the body needs. Though we have become civilized we know very little about food. Great strides have been made this century along specialized lines; first calories, then minerals and vitamins and enzymes. But haven't we lost sight of the wood for the trees? We still do not know how to combine them all, as nature does, to form a healthy body which will function perfectly for the normal span of life. If anyone doubts the effect of diet on health, beauty, and energy he should read *Let's Eat Right to Keep Fit*, Adelle Davis (Harcourt Brace & World, Inc., New York).

Modern man no longer walks. He hasn't the time. When obliged to get from one place to another a short distance away he (or especially she) is hampered by constricting clothes and shoes, or by carrying a heavy handbag, brief case, or parcels, so that instead of striding along fully using the muscles of his legs and lower trunk he puts one foot in front of the other using short steps and putting all his weight on his heels.

It would be interesting to ponder whether the wheel was not the beginning of man's physical decline. While walking, or riding horseback, he still used his muscles rewardingly. But sitting on something which pulled him along, his muscles began to degenerate and his joints to be jarred.

As transport became smoother, with proper roads and pneumatic tires, he began to slouch in a half-reclining position unaware that he needs to use his muscles not only to prevent himself from falling off a horse, a Roman chariot, or the top of a stagecoach, but also to diminish the vibration of modern transport. And now spaceships! What will the compression strain during the takeoff do for his spine?

Modern warfare has also caused much disc trouble, not so much by inflicting obvious wounds (which as well as causing fracture of bone, damage joints as well) but by tremendous explosions which, if they do not kill or do apparent damage to bodies, throw them about in fantastic positions, bring walls crashing down on them, force others to jump from tremendous heights to the ground or into the sea or lifeboat. These things have happened before but never on so vast a scale as in this century. It seems almost impossible for someone to have gone through modern warfare either as a combatant or civilian in a danger zone and not suffer damage which then or later resulted in disc lesion.

Modern furniture also takes its toll. Man surely invented furniture for his need and comfort so that it began by being functional. Nowadays, it rarely serves to support the body when tired, but is made to *look* comfortable to the masses who are trained by advertisement to believe it is so. Furniture designed to sit on is particularly to blame. (See "How to Sit.")

No doubt then modern man thinks himself more comfortable than his primitive ancestor. He is no longer nomadic, he lives in a sheltered house with furniture in which he slouches. He has a great variety of easily obtainable nonnutritious foods, which, although they make him overweight, he enjoys eating if his digestion will let him, and, when he does have to move from place to place, a choice of transport ranging from bumping along in a communal bus to flying through the air.

But let's face it. In comparison with his ancestors from primitive times to even a hundred years ago, he is physically degenerate. He has forfeited the satisfying feeling at the end of a day well spent in physical labor with perfect body coordination. His bones are still fairly sound but these have developed at expense of teeth and cartilage, and his muscles and ligaments are flabby and his nerves on edge.

Moreover, without sound cartilage, ligaments, and muscles he cannot expect to avoid disc trouble in his too heavy body; and with his nerves unduly sensitive he probably feels his pain with added intensity. Finally, disc lesions are by no means new. They have existed from the days of primitive man, but not until recently have been discovered or diagnosed as such.

In 1911 Goldthwait said he believed lumbago and sciatica came from disorders of the lumbosacral joint, but he did not know that this disorder was a disc protrusion.

In 1934 Mixter and Barr made a remarkable discovery. They removed part of the fifth lumbar disc to relieve a patient of sciatica. This was believed to be a *very rare* lesion.

In 1945 Cyriax proved that 90 percent of sciatica was caused by a disc lesion of the fifth or the fourth lumbar disc and that any lumbar disc could cause lumbago. He still did not suspect that disc lesions could occur in any level of the spine.

However, in 1948 he was able to show that cervical discs could act in the same way, causing torticollis (which is to the neck what lumbago is to the lower back) and later pain across the shoulder blades, or sometimes brachial neuritis.

Lastly, he was able to prove that "fibrositis" of the thoracic area, often later coming around to the front of the trunk as "intercostal neuritis" and sometimes imitating cardiac pain, was in many cases due to thoracic disc lesions at their various levels.

Though readily received in Europe, these discoveries are still not accepted by all medical men—nor is the quickest method of dealing with most of them, i.e. manipulation. This is because until recently only chiropractors and osteopaths manipulated at the spinal joints, claiming they could cure all diseases by manipulating back into position *misplaced vertebrae*. This unscientific claim set medical men against them, and against manipulation of the spinal joints.

It was left then for Cyriax to show that manipulations at the spinal joints could be used with great and speedy effect to reduce a recent *disc protrusion*, and many chronic ones as well.

Orthopedic men do not have the time for these sessions of manipulations. Physiotherapists are taught to do them. However, unfortunately the only place where they are taught at the present time is St. Thomas's Hospital, London, so that an orthopedic man who is interested in reducing a disc displacement instead of removing it must either send his assistants to train at St. Thomas's or have someone from there to teach his staff manipulation. This is not easy for him.

Although at St. Thomas's there are often visiting European physiotherapists learning these methods, there is a marked lack of students from the western side of the Atlantic. But the time will come when every orthopedic hospital will have its staff of physiotherapists for manipulation and traction.

When appendicitis was first diagnosed it too seemed a new "fashionable" disease, but that does not exclude the possibility that King John of England who supposedly died of a "surfeit of lampreys" did not in fact perish from a ruptured appendix. The picture of the village gaffer, bent over with his "rheumatics," more often than not provokes a kindly smile, but if told that the old man was really suffering from a slipped disc the onlooker would probably be quite concerned. "What's in a name?" The answer is perhaps rational, logical treatment, as against passive acceptance of a long life of half-health.

Conclusion

If you now ask "How did *I* get a slipped disc?" The answer is by doing too few of the correct things, and too many of the incorrect ones as explained in this book.

The understanding of anatomy of the disc is most important, otherwise you cannot see why you must or must not do certain things. The pressure of a disc not only causes pain, but many other symptoms.

If you are in treatment, you must do your part and not cancel the good effect of each session. If treatment by a physiotherapist is not possible, it is quite amazing how much you can help yourself by doing patiently and systematically the Corrective Movements on pages 23–27 at least three times a day, and more frequently when you are in pain or difficulty. The more often the better.

You must learn to lie with the spine in the normal alignment, properly supported, whether on your back or your side, and to avoid lying for long periods on the front.

When you sit, the buttocks should be well back, and you should sit upright unless the head and neck can be supported. Never sit with the legs stretched out in front.

You should learn to stand, so that the discs are centralized, and to walk without breaking them further.

Never bend with straight legs, and try to support the body while bending. Avoid lifting heavy weights.

Avoid increasing the compression strain on the spine by faulty positions, shocks, brusque movements, and unpleasant emotions. If the emotion is one of constant fear and depression which cannot be controlled, get the help of a psychiatrist. Make a point of lying down in the Supported Position for ten to fifteen minutes each day.

Do the simple exercises in Chapter 9 lying in the Supported Position, to strengthen the trunk muscles, especially the abdominals so that the discs are held in position.

When things go wrong help yourself in these ways:

1. Do the Corrective Movements, and repeat those of the neck with the weight of the head lifted off the body.

2. Take a really hot bath or shower or put hot compresses across the back of the neck or the lumbar curve as needed.

3. Repeat No. 1.

4. Lie in the Supported Position with a hot pad or bottle behind the neck or the lumbar curve, or both as the case may require, and in a relaxed atmosphere.

5. Take a hot drink or alcoholic drink or whatever relaxes you most.

6. Relieve any pressure in the bowels. An enema while sitting on the toilet is quick and efficient, and does not damage the muscles of the rectum.

7. Take an analgesic recommended by your doctor, or an effervescent tablet of calcium with Vitamin C 1000 mg., which can without harm be repeated every half hour until there is some relief from pain.

8. Try to relax with deep breathing. An ordinary inhaler such as that which is used when you have a cold is most helpful, especially if the pain is a headache.

9. The exercises in Chapter 9 may help relieve the pain.

No one wants to get old prematurely, and old age depends so much on the spine, from which pressure may interfere with the circulation, may cause stiffness in other joints, and great tiredness.

If you take care of your vertebral column, you will find that YOU ARE AS YOUNG AS YOUR SPINE.

Glossary

CALCIFICATION. Deposit of calcium. Bony formation.

CARTILAGE. Gristle found, e.g. lining joints, in outer ring of a disc, or in meniscus of the knee.

CERVICAL. Belonging to the neck.

CERVICAL CURVE. Nape of neck. (*See* Lordosis.)

CERVICAL LORDOSIS. Nape of neck. (*See* Lordosis.)

COMPRESSION STRAIN. Strain which squeezes a disc between two vertebrae by vertical pressure from above, e.g. carrying heavy weight; or from below, e.g. jumping on heels.

DISC. Rounded plaque or plate which acts as a shock absorber between two vertebrae.

DISC LESION. Damage of a disc: broken disc, slipped disc, disc with pulp protruding (Figs. 5, 6, 7, Chap. 1).

DISCOPATHY. Disc lesion or lesions (*disco* disc; *pathy* disease. Pronounced dis-cóp-athy).

DURA MATER. Thick covering surrounding brain and spinal cord.

FIBROCARTILAGENOUS RING. Outer ring of the disc made of cartilage and non-elastic fibrous tissue (Fig. 6, Chap. 1).

FLEXION. Act of bending forward. Opposite of extension.

GLUTEAL MUSCLES. Muscles of the buttock or rump on which one sits.

INTERVERTEBRAL DISC. (*See* Disc.)

JOINT. Articulation of two or more bones.

L-SHAPED POSITION. Seated position with the legs extended at 90 degrees to trunk, forming a capital L (Fig. 59, Chap. 4). To be avoided.

LAMINECTOMY. Operation for the removal of a disc.

LESION. Damage. (*See* Disc Lesion.)

LIGAMENT. Strong tough bands of fibrous and elastic tissue connecting bones together.

LORDOSIS. Curve as in cervical curve or lumbar curve (Fig. 4, Chap. 1). Used alone may mean exaggerated lumbar curve.

LUMBAR. Belonging to lower part of back.

LUMBAR CURVE. Small of back. (*See* Lordosis.)

LUMBAR LORDOSIS. (*See* Lordosis.)

PROTRUDING DISC. Slipped disc. Disc of which part protrudes beyond the rim of the vertebrae which enclose it.

SLIPPED DISC. (*See* Protruding Disc.)

SUPPORTED POSITION. Lying position on bed or couch in which the neck, small of back, and knees are supported (Fig. 22, Chap. 3).

THORACIC. Belonging to the Thorax.

THORAX. Part of trunk between neck and lower back.

VERTEBRAE. Segments which make up the spine (Fig. 2, Chap. 1).

VERTEBRAL COLUMN. Spine.